W9-DEJ-668

DATE DUE

HIGHSMITH #45115

THE

KEBRA

NAGAST

■

**EDITED BY
GERALD HAUSMAN**

**INTRODUCTION BY
ZIGGY MARLEY**

■

St. Martin's Press

New York

THE
KEBRA
NAGAST

The Lost Bible of Rastafarian

Wisdom and Faith from

Ethiopia and Jamaica

Design by Songhee Kim

Library of Congress Cataloging-in-Publication Data

Kebra Nagast. English. Selections.
    The Kebra Nagast : the lost bible of Rastafarian wis-
  dom and faith from Ethiopia and Jamaica / edited by
  Gerald Hausman.—1st ed.
        p.   cm.
    ISBN 0-312-16793-8
    1. Rastafari movement.   2. Kebra Nagast—Criti-
  cism, interpretation, etc.   3. Spiritual life.   4. Conduct
  of life.   5. Jamaica—Religious life and customs.   6.
  Ethiopia—Religious life and customs.   I. Hausman,
  Gerald.   II. Title.
  BL2532.R37K43   1997
  299'.676—dc21   97-18817
                                                      CIP

7   9   10   8

CONTENTS

INTRODUCTION

This book is about the mind. It is about black history, my history, black my story. But you must see the way words can mislead because this book is not "his story," but our story. When I was in school I used to think a lot about the English language and how words are used in ways that are not always what we think. History, "his story," words like "di-ed" and "liv-ed." The word for lived should be "livity." We live; that is all.

In school, when we were taught of the slave trade, we did not hear of the glory of the kings and the Kebra Nagast. We heard about "his story." We did not hear of African glory, black my story, the truth as revealed in the Kebra Nagast. We came to realize that even the Bible is just a version of the truth, and all of these versions are a part of the whole, a vision of what happened, is happening, and will happen.

My father said, "It's the last quarter before the year 2000, and righteousness—the positive way of thinking—must win." As I see it, the year 2000 is based on a Roman system of time measurement. The original counting of time, calendar days, months, and years, is not even near 2,000 yet. So the real calendar should have more significance, be rooted in spirituality, rooted in God-belief. I don't personally celebrate the New Year or Christmas, and each time is just time that continues along. The sun comes up, the sun goes down. Every day.

What my father said, though, is prophecy. There is no way the negative can ultimately conquer. When the whole battle, the whole war, is won, it will be good things that prosper; goodness must prosper in the end.

Sometimes people think there is a magical reality in the things that we write, or say, or do, as when these lines of mine were written:

> Above my bed, Bob's face I saw, my
>   daddy
> looking at me so passionately, little
>   brother.
> Well, in his eyes I saw the truth, mommy,
> the truth of a Rastaman,
> the truth of a iyaman.

We understand, however, that things must come, and we have to let them out, let them happen. Not supernatural experience but inspiration and vision: real, not magical. At times I wonder if I myself have some knowledge of things beyond my existence, but I don't think too deep, just lightly. The spirit lives on. The spiritual sense will always be here, as the music will be here; my father's music lives as he lives in the music.

I was born at home in Trenchtown. And the experience

of the ghetto in those days, when I was coming up, was not the same as what my father experienced in terms of the violence and the mind-set of the people. My life didn't have sufferation. We did not go through the same things that my father went through, but it's not only physical experience that makes you what you are: Jah gives the inspiration and my music is based more upon a spiritual level than a physical one. The music comes from Jah, but I use my own inner eye, my third eye, to make the music. If it takes another century for people to understand, it is all right. I don't rush it. I wait.

If a song makes sense, it will always be there for people to understand. Sometime, some way, somehow, they will get the message. Maybe not in the time that we expect, or want. But the work that we're doing is not just for now. It is for all time. Naturally, you may doubt and question (it's all right to do so), but when I think of Jesus Christ, Marcus Garvey, my father—who am I to complain or question? Jesus Christ suffered so much—if I get a little doubt, it means so little.

A couple of years ago a reporter asked me, "Will you live to see the freedom of South Africa?" and I answered, "Of course." My generation is a positive generation, and there's so much more to go, as the self is changing. Most important, the human creature needs to evolve into a loving creature. I mean, if you don't love, what are you?

But we can never stop the struggle. I have dreams for the upliftment of my people, but I am not at the point where I can reach the fulfillment of my dreams. Still, the struggle cannot be taken away; it was not given to us, it was born in us. And it runs through our veins and creates the urge to help people. It was not something that I read in a book, or heard from a friend. I was always this way. So no matter where I live, or what fame comes to me (these things can be taken away—money comes, money goes), the struggle is always in the blood.

Each person must go through his own tribulations until spiritual enlightenment takes place—until he sees love of life, love of self, love of tree, love of bird, love of bee. Everybody has to go through this. But to those who see me perform, I am perhaps only a thought in their minds. They see what they want to see, not knowing what I have been through in order to reach the place that I have come to.

So it's not just my father that made me what I am—it's me as well. And people who see me sing cannot see the struggle that is behind the words that I sing. And it's as I said in the beginning, it is all in the mind, like the calendar of our beginnings. And these words here, now. Jah said to me, "Don't worry about what you are going to say. Don't worry, the words will come."

And like the words in the Kebra Nagast, they come in their own time.

—Ziggy Marley

PREFACE

Solomon, the King, ruled over Judah and Israel nearly three thousand years ago. Although he has been called the wisest man who ever lived because of his fairness as a ruler and his virtue as a king, he was also a historian, an orator, a poet, one who knew the importance of the word. He was mainly, however, a man of God whose only failing, as history would have it, was his passion for women and his desire to sow his seed so that his line might continue forever. This drive of Solomon's forced him, as nothing else did, to disobey the Lord, and thus to herald the fall of his empire.

Solomon's hubris, his tragic flaw, is the meat and bone of the Ethiopian bible, the Kebra Nagast, which, translated, is "the glory of the kings." In this work, unlike the King James Bible, we see King Solomon struggling with his own mortality. We see him stripped of pretension, desperately in search of what he has, through his disobedience to God, lost. Yet his great passion gained him a son whose destiny matches his own. Bayna-Lehkem, or David, as he is called by Solomon (because of the boy's likeness to his grandfather, King David), is a man of virtue, who will further Solomon's work and extend his glory to Ethiopia.

So, Solomon's weakness for women, which brings about

his dissolution and threatens the ruin of his empire, gives him the thing he is truly seeking: a son to walk in his own footsteps, a son wiser, by dint of his virtue, than himself.

The Kebra Nagast shows Solomon's loss, as well as his gain. For it shows how Solomon is disinherited by the Lord when he marries the daughter of the pharaoh and worships her golden insect idols. For this he is punished severely, and we discern, not only in the Kebra Nagast but in the Bible, his absolute nihilism. Brought to his knees by God, Solomon discovers that knowledge is nothing more than sorrow. His ultimate disillusionment ("For in much wisdom is much grief: and he that increaseth knowledge increaseth sorrow") is the bitter nutmeat of Ecclesiastes. Solomon's only joy at the end of his career as king, according to the Kebra Nagast, is his belief that Bayna-Lehkem, his Ethiopian son, will out-shine his own accomplishments and bring greater glory to a new Solomonic line of kings.

By whom, we might ask, did Solomon acquire a son from the land of Ethiopia? Of course, the answer is the Queen of Sheba. She was, by all reports, a black woman, the Queen of the South, whose home country was in the southern part of Assyria. She was named Makeda, Sheba being only the country of her birth. According to legend, she possessed her own share of mysticism and power, a willing match for the omniscient Solomon. The Kebra Nagast gives us reason to believe that Makeda studied Solomon's wisdom and integrity as a ruler and brought it to Ethiopia. Then, having borne Solomon a son, she waited until the appropriate time and turned over the affairs of state to him, granting him all of her powers.

What is interesting about this particular history is that it supports what certain scholars describe as the legitimate claim of blackness in biblical lore. The idea is not new. The Solomonic line, according to myth, is "mixed," and thus black people in the Bible, as well as in Coptic literature, are, indeed, among our most famous patriarchal and matriarchal figures. Moses, for example, was said to be the husband of a Cushite woman. Makeda was certainly black. Ham, the son of Noah, was said to be black. Theological scholar Reverend Walter Arthur McCray (*The Black Presence in the Bible*) writes: "The existence and experiences of ancient Black/African people are recorded in the Bible. The Bible contains a substantial amount of information written by black people, about them, and, in many cases, addressed specifically to them." Indeed, it is more than likely that the mixed multitude of Exodus included blacks and that Egyptians, Syrians, and Hebrews (and other native peoples of biblical times) were not just dark of skin, but black in feature as well. And what was Israel, in the time of Solomon, if not a group of indeterminate nations, including a great many people of color?

The claim of the Kebra Nagast is that God favored and loved the people of Ethiopia because they did not reject the Son of Man when he walked on earth. They, the text states, beheld and loved their savior. However, the richest claim of all is that of the Ark of the Covenant, and this is the heart of the Kebra Nagast, and the thing that makes it a document of such inordinate fascination. Much of the text deals with the removal of the Ark from the Temple by Bayna-Lehkem and its subsequent enshrinement in Ethiopia. According to the myth told here, the Ethiopians were guided by God's angels, who enabled them to remove the Ark and carry it to Ethiopia. Legend holds that it resides there to this day.

The text of this edition of the Kebra Nagast was selected from a portion of a book entitled *The Queen of Sheba and Her Only Son Menyelek*. First published in English in 1922, the translator, Dr. E. A. Wallis Budge, was Scholar of Christ's College, Cambridge. He was also the Tyrwhitt Hebrew Scholar at Christ's College and Keeper of Egyptian and Assyrian Antiquities at the British Museum. Of the book Dr. Budge wrote: "The Kebra Nagast is a great storehouse of legends and traditions, some historical and some of purely folklore character, derived from the Old Testament and the later Rabbinic writings, and from Egyptian (both pagan and Christian), Arabian, and Ethiopic sources. Of the early history of the compilation and its maker, and of its subsequent editors we know nothing, but the principal groundwork of its earliest form was the traditions that were current in Syria, Palestine, Arabia, and Egypt during the first four centuries of the Christian era." Dr. Budge indicates that the earliest form of the text, written in Ge'ez, or Ethiopic, appeared around the sixth century C.E. The compiler was probably a Coptic priest. Subsequently, the text was translated into Arabic. Then, in the fourteenth century, the Kebra Nagast was once again translated into Ethiopic by a Christian visionary, of whom little is known except that his name was Isaac, and that he was an Ethiopian patriot. His personal statement on the translation is as follows: "I have toiled much for the glory of the kingdom of Ethiopia, and for the going forth of the heavenly Zion, and for the glory of the king of Ethiopia."

So the Kebra Nagast is a work of centuries-old revisions and translations from Ethiopic to Arabic and back again to Ethiopic, and from thence to English. German and French translations of the book also appeared in the late nineteenth and early twentieth centuries. There have been no accessible English translations since 1922, with the exception of a text published in Jamaica by Miguel F. Brooks that was compiled, edited, and translated from Arabic, French, and Spanish sources.

My own interest in the Kebra Nagast came about as I heard stories from it when I spoke to Rastafarians, most of whom had not read it, but all of whom knew of it. One man in particular knew the book quite well and told me that he had learned the stories through the Ethiopian Orthodox Church in Jamaica. Then a piece of luck brought a copy of the Kebra Nagast into my own hands. A Jamaican Rastafarian living in Miami had found a copy of the book in an abandoned apartment; the copy was a Xerox of Dr. Budge's translation (the only extant copies of which are at the British Museum and in some private collections).

Here was a copy of the book that I could read; moreover there were copious marginal notes, and even indications by a Rastafarian brother on which chapters and which passages were relevant to his own studies. Using these notes and following my own instincts as a storyteller, I selected the histories of patriarchs and kings whose names figure prominently in the Old Testament. My emphasis, of course, was on Solomon because his name was on the lips of the Rastas whom I interviewed.

Dr. Budge states in his preface that the words he chose for the first English edition of the Kebra Nagast were as close to the original text as he could get them. But what was the original text? We have to assume that it was at best an oral history composed over many hundreds of years and re-composed, at will, by anyone so inclined. What is remarkable about the book is that its dissemination has remained, even now, at the threshold of the twenty-first century, mostly oral.

My expertise is in traditional or native storytelling. In working on the Kebra Nagast I have held in mind two things: the way Dr. Budge translated stories and the way my Jamaican Rastafarian friends spoke them. Poetry was in the latter, thematic exactitude in the former. Between the two I found common ground, however, as I would hear the stories, then read them; afterwards, I would study the King James Bible and the Koran for further echoes and illuminations. Then, too, I had the notes of an unknown but assiduous Rastafarian scholar to help me on my way. All of these exercises became part of the process of selecting the text which appears in the present volume.

The stories that follow these portions of the Kebra Nagast explore the philosophical faith of the Rastafarian brotherhood in Jamaica. We started this informal study, my wife, Lorry, and I, in the summer of 1986 and concluded it in the summer of 1996. The writing is based on roving interviews with Rastas, who were at first friends, and finally family, as our daughter married a Jamaican.

I am obliged by the Rastafarian community to mention that this work is not a story, but rather, in their words, a history. What it contains, of course, comes from the spoken tradition; histories, in the oldest of African traditions, do not have to be written in order to be proven accurate. They are told. This, then, is a telling, not a retelling, though, because even the first appearance of the Kebra Nagast was a retelling. That there is no "original" text is not a problem for the Rastafarian, for all words, all utterances come "from Creation." Every human syllable is an announcement of humankind upon the earth, of the "I" walking through time, which is the Mount Zion moment, now.

THE HISTORIC IMPLICATIONS
OF THE KEBRA NAGAST

The cultural heritage of the Kebra Nagast is not merely Ethiopian, but is universally African. As Jamaican author I. Jabulani Tafari (*A Rastafari View of Marcus Mosiah Garvey*) writes, "The origins of Ethiopian/Egyptian civilization go back into remote antiquity to the predawn of history over five thousand years ago. Ethiopia (the predecessor of Egypt) predates even the building of the biblical Tower of Babel by Nimrod and the founding of ancient Babylon by the Sumerians. Likewise, the pyramid (for which Egypt is famous), as a mystical and scientific symbol and also as a practical architectural design and building structure, goes back to the beginning of recorded time and to the Ethiopian roots of world culture in Kemet. The Cushites were the world's first brick and stone masons. Their expertise can be seen by the Great Pyramid at Giza, which remained the largest and tallest building in the world for over four thousand years until modern times. All this explains why Cushite Egypt was the first known world power in recorded history."

Upon the foundation of such thinking, Marcus Mosiah Garvey, the Jamaican liberator, created an Ethiopian/African movement, both political and religious, that is with us now.

During the 1920s he resurrected the concept of the African origin of civilization and he recast the African race as members of an elite society which he termed "noble Ethiopians." All African people, whether Afro-American or Afro-Caribbean, or simply African, were a part of what Garvey believed was the coming of a new order for black people the world over. Referring to his own roots as Ethiopian, Garvey instituted the concept of black pride, and is credited with the first modern oratorical use of "black is beautiful."

Moreover, it was Marcus Garvey who also quoted Psalm 68:31: "Princes shall come out of Egypt; Ethiopia shall soon stretch her hands unto Jah." In general, Garvey was speaking about history, but, in particular, he was making reference to Ras Tafari, Emperor Haile Selassie I, the last of the Solomonic line of kings to be seated on an Ethiopian throne. In so doing, perhaps unconsciously, he released the seed that would grow into a religion, beginning in the 1930s and extending to the present time. This religion is, of course, Rastafari.

The tenets of Rasta are buried deep in the Old Testament, but they have more in common with the Kebra Nagast than with the King James Bible. The authorized King James Bible, which first appeared in 1611, was, according to Brooks's version of the Kebra Nagast, going to include this Ethiopian work. However, the editors were told, presumably by the clergy—although it came down by royal decree—to excise the chapters which included the Kebra Nagast. Although this might seem a bit peculiar, it made sense from the point of view of religion. At any rate, it is unmistakable that Jesus Christ, linked to the line of King Solomon, was a man of color. Furthermore, as stated earlier, the entire text of the Kebra Nagast is a paean to the Ethiopian people, the "chosen ones," the book says. These were, states the Kebra Nagast, the people who were given the Ark of the Covenant by God's own angels. The book's claim for greatness must be legitimate, for if it were not, the text would not have been suppressed by European and African monarchs alike; nor would it have languished in the British Museum for over seventy years. In fact, the Zagwe (also spelled Zâguê) kings of Ethiopia, who were not in the Solomonic line, were themselves suppressors of the book. So for more than a thousand years, this history of Ethiopia has awaited the readership it deserves. Let us hope that we are ready to read it with an unbiased eye, today, at the cusp of the twenty-first century.

THE
KEBRA
NAGAST

EARTH

I The Father, the Son, and the Holy Spirit together fashioned Zion, which is the Kingdom of Heaven. And they said, "Let us make Man in our likeness."

The Son said, "I will wear the body of Adam."

And the Holy Spirit said, "I will dwell in the heart of the righteous."

And the Father said, "I will become Man and I will abide in everything I create. I will dwell in flesh as well as seed and plant; and I will dwell in air as well as water; and I will dwell in earth."

Now in the days thereafter, through the pleasure of the Father, there came the Second Zion whose name was Jesus Christ.

But let us speak of how it was in the beginning.

II Adam was king of all that the Father created, but he was driven out of the Garden because of the sin of the Serpent, which was the plan of Satan. Now when Cain was born, Adam saw that he was sullen-faced and bad-tempered, and he was sad at the sight of this. And then Abel was born and Adam saw that he was good-tempered, and that his face was also good. So Adam spoke out and said, "This is my son, the heir of my kingdom."

Now Satan was envious of Abel and he cast this envy into the heart of Cain, where it grew. Cain remembered the words of his father, saying that

Abel would be the heir of his throne. And he thought of the sister who had been born with Cain and who had a beautiful face; and this sister was given by Adam to Abel. And he thought of the sister who had been born with Abel and whose face was unlovely; and this sister was given by Adam to Cain. And these things grew like a seed of envy in the heart of Cain. But there was yet another thing that caused him to be angry with his brother, for the offerings that were made by each of the brothers were not accepted equally by Adam; Adam accepted Abel's sacrifice and rejected Cain's.

So envy rose up in the heart of Cain and because of this he struck his brother and killed him. Afterwards, however, he understood what he had done and trembled over it, and he was then driven away by Adam and the Father.

Now when Seth was born Adam looked upon him and knew that the Father had shown compassion: "He hath given to me the light of my face." And the birth of Seth destroyed the name of the one who slayed his heir.

III From Adam until Noah, there passed ten generations. And all during this time, the generations of Cain also propagated and made of themselves a lawless breed that cared nothing for the grace of godliness, the love of the Father. They lived for themselves and they paid no homage to the Father, and, at length, they put the seed of the ass into the mare, bringing the mule into being, which the Father had not commanded in any way.

Noah, however, was a righteous man. And he was the tenth generation from Adam. He told his children not to mingle with the children of Cain, for these children were filled with exultant pride, boastful speech, and false oaths. And man wrought sexual wickedness with man, and woman wrought sexual wickedness with woman.

Thus did the Father let loose the waters of the Flood, and the children of Cain reaped the fruit of their corruption, and with them went all beasts and creeping things. These had been created for Adam to provide food and pleasure, but they were now, for his sake, destroyed. What remained were eight souls and seven of every kind of clean beast and creeping thing, and two of every kind of unclean beast and creeping thing.

IV Now before Noah died, he called forth his three sons, Shem, Ham, and Japheth. To Shem, he said: "Be God to thy brother." To Ham, "Be servant to thy brother." And to Japheth, "Be servant to Shem, my heir."

Noah's order was obeyed, but this did not stop the Devil's hostility against the children of Noah. After the flood, the Devil stirred up Canaan, the son of Ham. And Canaan took the kingdom from the children of Shem; and again brother rose up against brother.

While Noah lived he saw the kingdom divided, and he prayed to the Father, "If you destroy the earth with a second flood, blot me out with those who perish."

But the Father said, "I will make a covenant with you. Tell your children not to eat the beast that has died of itself; nor one that has been torn apart by wild beasts. Tell them not to cultivate harlotry, and I, on my part, will not destroy the earth a second time with a flood, but will give your children seed time and harvest time, and the four seasons that bring these into being."

And the Father said further to Noah: "My covenant will be with your children forever because I have sworn it, by myself and by Zion, the tabernacle of my covenant, which I have made for the salvation of all men. And when they see a cloud upon the sky, they will not fear it, nor think it danger unto them, as in the coming of another flood; for they will see the bow of my covenant, which will henceforth be known as a rainbow, the crown of my law. And this crown will remind the children that, even though their sins may multiply, their trust in me will be ever in place, because I shall not be angry with them, but will put away my anger and send them my compassion. So even if heaven and earth pass away, my word shall not pass away."

I Terah, who lived eight generations after Shem, had a son whose name was Abram,* and on the boy's twelfth birthday his father sent him off to sell idols.

Abram told him, "These cannot make deliverance." He took them as he was told, but made no effort to sell them. To those who would buy them, he asked, "Do you wish to buy artificial idols made of wood, stone, and brass?"

And the people, hearing the words of the boy, passed by the idols with disdain. Returning home, Abram placed the idols on the roadside and he spoke to them, saying, "Can you deliver me bread to eat or water to drink?"

None of the idols answered him, and they remained silent. So Abram defiled them with his feet, kicking the face of one and smashing the body of another until all lay in pieces by the road, and he said to them, "If you cannot defend yourselves from harm, how can you defend me?"

Then Abram turned his face towards heaven and cried, "Oh, maker of the universe; creator of sun, moon, sea, and earth; maker of that which is seen and that which is not seen, from this

*Abram is the spelling used for Abraham in the Kebra Nagast.

day forth I will place myself in your care."

After saying this, Abram saw a chariot of fire come into view and he was afraid, and he fell to the ground and shielded his eyes. Then he heard a voice which spoke to him and said, "Give up your fear and stand upright."

So the Father removed fear from him and the Father placed his blessing upon Abram and said there was now a covenant between them: "I will bring down the Tabernacle of my covenant seven generations after you and your seed shall be the salvation of the race." Then the Father spoke against the kinsmen of Abram, saying that they were worshipers of idols, and he told Abram to leave the land of his fathers and go to a new land which he would show to him.

So Abram went to the home of his father and he took his wife, Sarah, and they went forth and did not return to his father, mother, or the land of his kinsmen. But he went to the city of Salem and there reigned in righteousness, and the Father blessed him greatly, and he died an honorable man with a large kingdom of his own.

II Now it came to pass that Moses, who was of the seed of Abram, was told by the Father to make a likeness of his law as it was brought down to earth. The Father said, "Make an Ark of wood that cannot be eaten by worms and overlay it with pure gold, and upon this, place the word of the law, which is the covenant written by my own hand."

And the Tabernacle is a spiritual thing, full of compassion; it is a heavenly thing, full of light, it is a thing of freedom, and a habitation of the Father. And the work thereof is marvelous, and it resembles jasper, topaz, hyacinthine stone, and the crystal and the light catch the eye by force; and it astonishes the mind, for it was made by the mind of God. Within it are the manna from heaven that came down to earth and the rod of Aaron that sprouted after it withered, though no one watered it with water.

Moses covered the Ark with pure gold and made poles to carry it and rings to hold them, and he made the people of Israel see it and carry it to the land of their inheritance which was the city of Jerusalem, the city of Zion. When they were crossing the Jordan and the priests were carrying it, the waters stood up like a wall and did not topple or fall.

And prophets were appointed over the people of Israel in the Tabernacle of Testimony, where the priests and the people redeemed themselves from sin by placing offerings. Moses and his brother Aaron were instructed to make holy vessels for the Tabernacle. And these things were gold pitchers, embroidered cloths, candlesticks and bowls, crowns and carpets, hangings of silk and the red hides of rams, hyacinthine and purple hangings, sardius stones, sapphires and emeralds.

And all of these offerings of gold and silver and silk were to be placed in the Tabernacle of the Law, an Ark of wood uneaten and uneatable by worms, and these were to reside along with the two tablets written by the fingers of the Father, which were to have been preserved in enameled gold so that the Law might be protected and carried.

In all of this was Moses commanded on Mount Sinai: the pattern of the tent that would cover all, and how it was to be cut and the work thereof. And

Zion was revered and the Father came down on the mountain and spoke with his chosen ones; and he opened the door of salvation to them, and he delivered them from their enemies.

And the Father spoke from the pillar of cloud and commanded the people to keep his law and walk with him in the ways he had set forth.

In Jamaica references to the Bible and the Kebra Nagast can be seen in the patterns of everyday life. Some say the John Canoe or Jonkonnu celebration—part dance and part pantomime—at Christmastime is Noah's Ark and, at the same time, the Ark of the Covenant. In the Bible Jacob's ladder refers to the pathway to heaven used by the angels as Jacob slept beneath it and dreamed. The Jacob's Ladders of Jamaica, however, are cut into formidable cliff rock or clay, and they are reportedly used by fallen as well as risen angels. The words John Canoe *may come from the Ewe language of Eastern Ghana and Togo, where* dzonu kunu *meant sorcerer.*

The old men walking along the ziggy Jamaican roads, wearing tall black rubber boots, coming home in the evening, fierce-faced and fiery-eyed, remind Ernie that it's better to be on the move than to be still somewhere. "For, after all," he comments as we round the turn towards Oracabessa, where he grew up, "a man is like water; if he slows down or stops, he becomes stagnant." He says this in patois, "Walk fe nuttin' better than siddung fe nuttin'." We have a large laugh over this perfect expression of truth, and how it betters the English version by far.

We drive into the little seaport town where the banana was once king and the men of Oracabessa sang original choruses of "The Banana Boat Song" while bearing green bunches on their backs; banana ferriers tossing huge bunches, from man to man, from the shore to ship.

The best of these banana carriers was Ernie's father.

Ernie stops the car and points out the cliff edge over which we can see the old harbor where the men had once toiled, glistening with sweat.

"Look now, there's the Jacob's Ladder," Ernie says, chuckling. Here on the reef-rock hill, a brave and giant fig tree has made its stand, sending cabled roots to the beach bottom far below.

"Many times," Ernie says, "I stood at the top of the Jacob's Ladder, waiting for my father. You see the steps carved in the hill? The men used the vines as ropes and they used the earth steps to steady their feet as they hung in the air and drew themselves up. That's why they called it Jacob's Ladder."

We stare down the hill into the dappled emerald shade, and I remember the story in Genesis where Jacob dreamed of a ladder that extended to heaven, with angels ascending and descending.

Ernie continues ruefully, "My father was a devilish man. He spent his money on gambling, playing poker and bone dice on the dock when he got off work. My sister, Merline, waited all day down there, hoping for sixpence, or tuppence, from our father, who everybody knew as Brother John."

Laughing at the memory, Ernie goes on, "But he was a trickster, Brother John. He'd sneak through the lines of men with his money in his pocket. Then he'd come up the Jacob's Ladder before Merline could see him, and he'd sneak away. And for what? To spend the rest of the day gambling. Drinking rum and gambling. I saw him. Yes, I saw him down there, even though Merline didn't."

Ernie's father's tale is not unusual on an island where poverty destroys more families than the wars of the heart. In Jamaica, hope springs eternal but jobs are few. Ernie bears no malice, however, towards the father who didn't raise him; for Brother John, who abandoned him along with his two sisters and three brothers.

"It happened in a day," he explains. "In one day, we lost it all."

Ernie drops back into patois, as he recalls those long gone days when he was a child. "Him get mix up wid obeah woman. She gi' de mon a potion a obeah oil, what dey call 'gone fe good, come fe stay.' Dat lady live next door to we, so one day Breddah John him go fe her house fe live. 'Im just packed up him ting, and gone fe good. Yes, de Devil took Breddah John."

He laughs and adds, "It's really true because he was a John Canoe man. Brother John played the part of the Devil. I, the little boy, was the Devil's Treasurer."

The John Canoe is a wild street dance put on at or just before Christmas in Jamaica. It included six main characters. There was the Bosun, a big fat short man, honking and oinking and making people laugh; the King and the Queen, spurious royalty; the Horse, wearing a hobbyhorse headdress costume, rocking up a storm; the Indian, solemn; and the Policeman, foolish, helpless, always asserting his authority. All these people gesturing and dancing.

"The big star of John Canoe was the Devil, played by my father, Brother John." Ernie says that Brother John took this devil's work seriously; more seriously than he took his life. He played the role so well, in fact, that, as time went on, he forgot it was a role at all.

"My father," Ernie remarks, "was really the Devil. Yes, he became the Devil incarnate. Then he didn't need his costume anymore."

One afternoon when Brother John got home from the dock, the obeah, or voodoo woman invited him to her kitchen for some callaloo soup. And into that hot, peppery soup, she poured a libation of obeah oil. After that, he was hers. She knew it, and so did Ernie's family. So it was up to his mother, who had no job, to try and figure out what to do.

The road to Tank Lane where Brother John left his family more than thirty years ago is a short but steep trip up from the harbor road of Oracabessa. The earth is red there, rich and red like blood. The flowering trees that sprout from it are paradisiacal: guinep, breadfruit, grapefruit, june plum, bougainvillea, croton, pimento. The air is sweet with those good-smelling trees, and cardamom-scented, moist earth, and the bittersweet smell, somewhere, of burning leaf trash. The yards are small and clean, the dirt swept to an immaculate patina. The houses, neat and trim, come from the Victorian era. Many of them have rusted zinc roofs and yards where roosters scuttle about monitoring hens. The breadfruit trees hang with bursting fruit and the Jamaican cherries sparkle. Banana fronds, lazy and liquid in their turning from side to side, give the day an idle cast, a falsity that everything is easy.

"Brother John left us to this," Ernie says, switching back into English. "Somewhere between the Devil and the deep blue sea."

We laugh at this, but Ernie's laughter soon fades.

"You don't see John Canoe dancers like those in my father's time. That is all gone, along with the banana men, the banana songs, and the shillings and pence of payday."

In the eighteenth century the John Canoe dancers commemorated Noah's Flood by transporting a representation of the Ark upon their heads. The Ark itself was a symbol of the world's destruction and resurrection, a huge and towering commemoration of the ancient myth from the Bible and the Kebra Nagast.

Today the old Ark can still be seen at the John Canoe in Ocho Rios, Jamaica. An old man who wears it is known as "Tree" and he comes down the main street, his head and upper body all but buried in a fabulous ark of green, woven of ferns, fronds, and hibiscus flowers. Some say that Tree is the last member of an old mummer's group, where the dancer who bore the ark of flowers was a character called Jock-O-Green. Nineteenth-century engravings show this dancer wearing a huge bower of palm leaves, which, no doubt, is something of Solomon's Ark of the Covenant, Noah's Ark, and the Christmas mummery of the British Isles all rolled into one.

Ernie reaches for the faded photograph of Brother John that he keeps in the visor of his car. So, here is Brother John: wearing a suit too small for him, his long arms hanging nearly to his knees. He looks awkward and odd, gangly and misshapen.

"I am glad I have this little picture," says Ernie, smiling. "For that is all I have of Brother John."

In spite of everything—the suffering his family had to endure without his father, the hard poverty they had to deal with each and every day—Ernie says he still owes his father a lot of respect.

"He put me on the path to Rastafari," he says. "From the time when I first accepted my responsibilities, I was Rasta. I learned about my faith the hard way, through work and sufferation, and through the help of elders who were not my father. But even from afar, and offering no help at all, Brother John disapproved. This made me stand up for what I believed. And it made me a man, a righteous man, a Rasta. He didn't try to understand my dealing with Rastafari. Instead, he tried to feed me pork, and other things that we Rastas don't eat, when I came to visit him. That is what made me strong, that opposition. And, of course, my love for him." And, in his own way, Ernie believes, Brother John loved him too.

"Would he have let me hold his purse? Would he have let me be his treasurer, if he didn't trust me? In trust, you know, is love. Yes, Brother John did love his son Ernie. Give thanks and praise to the Almighty for that."

I Samson was of the seed of Dan, one of the twelve sons of Jacob. Now the Angel of the Lord appeared to the mother of Samson and said, "Keep yourself pure and keep to the bed of your husband, for the one who shall be born of you will deliver Israel from the hand of the Philistines."

And then she brought forth Samson.

And again the Angel appeared and said to her, "Let no razor go upon his head; neither shall he eat flesh nor drink wine. Nor shall he marry a strange woman, but only a woman of his own kin and from the house of his father."

Now the Father gave Samson strength in abundance, but in time he disobeyed the Father's law: he married Delilah, the daughter of a Philistine. God became angry with him then and delivered him into the hands of his enemies, who blinded him and made him act the fool in the house of their king. And Samson pulled the roof down upon them, and killed 700,000 of them as if they were so many locusts. And Samson died in the ruin he had wrought with his own strength; but his death was an honorable one.

II And Delilah was with child, but Samson was no more. Now when this boy was born he was given the name Menahem, which means "seed of the strong man." Delilah was the sister of Maksaba, who was the wife of the Philistine king whom Samson had killed. The dominion of the king was gone, ruined by Samson, but it had now fallen into the hands of Maksaba.

And then Maksaba brought forth a man-child and the two women, having a love for one another that surpassed even the love of sisters, decided to raise their children together. And in time the people seated the son of Maksaba on the throne of his father and made him King of the Philistines. Now in time the son of Samson asked his mother why he was not sitting upon the throne. And she explained to him that it did not belong to his father, and the city was not his father's city.

And he replied, "I will neither forsake you, my mother, nor Maksaba my mother, and I will be King here." One day the two youths were drunk and the son of Delilah had taken a large piece of roasted meat, and the son of Maksaba took away a piece that hung from his mouth. Menahem then drew his sword and cut off the head of his rival, whose body fell heavily upon the paving stones of the house. When the two mothers saw this, they did not know what to do.

And Delilah rose up and seized the sword of the dead son of her sister. And now Menahem hid behind a pillar and prepared to kill his own mother. So Maksaba seized Delilah and said, "This youth has sprung from a bad root which cannot bear good fruit. Come, my sister, do not let him destroy you also." And then Maksaba spoke soothingly to Menahem, who raged like a bear. In truth he wished to kill both women, but instead he made them leave the palace.

After he himself left the palace, the two women came back and prepared the dead body for burial, and they buried it secretly.

When the time for the evening meal had come, the servants sought their king and could not find him. So Maksaba said to them, "Your king is sick, but Menahem will sit in his place." From that time onward the son of Samson reigned over the Philistines, and fifteen winters had passed since the time he was born and the time that he committed his act of murder.

The natural man, rootsman, rastamon, unchained by technolog-
ical civilization, is the ideal role of all Rastas. Some of the more
reactionary members of the brotherhood, those who might be
termed extremely "rootical" rather than extremely radical, shun
all eating utensils which are made of "the metals of Babylon"
and they hold their dreadlocks as a covenant that concretizes their
faith and goes back to the codes in the Old Testament and the
Kebra Nagast. Some Rastas refer to the myth of Samson, blind,
baldheaded, and chained to the pillars of the Philistine palace as
an example of what can happen when one loses the locks under
the hand of artifice; when one trusts a wicked woman; and when
one refuses to honor the will of Jah. Eyeless in Gaza, Samson is
the symbol of paradise lost and found. For, as it says in the Kebra
Nagast and the Bible (Judges 13:9–14), an angel appeared before
the mother of Samson, and said: "Thou shalt not let a razor go
upon his head, and he shall neither eat flesh nor drink wine, and
he shall marry no strange woman but only a woman of his own
kin and from the house of his father."

One of the primary codes of the traditional Rasta is to keep
the locks from comb, scissors, or razor. This stems directly
from the old Hebraic laws of nondefilement, as reaffirmed

by members of the Ethiopian National Congress: "We strongly object to sharp implements used in the desecration of the Figure of Man; e.g., trimming and shaving, tattooing of the skin, and cutting of the flesh."

The name Samson is sacred to Rastafarians in Jamaica because he is the legendary locksman whose power ebbed away when he lost his hair. Once Delilah was done with him, Samson suffered the fate of the archetypal man whose weakness is woman. This is a paradigm all Rastas understand. There is, in fact, an old reggae tune with the verse, "The woman is like a shadow; the man is like an arrow," about female subversiveness. Nor is this myth confined to the Bible, the Koran, or the Kebra Nagast. It is also an African precept built upon many old African tales of man's undoing.

Samson was a man who could snap a bowstring like a piece of thread, but after Delilah cuts off his hair he is rendered helpless as a babe. In Gaza, where he has been carried away, blinded by his enemies, the Philistines, he is taunted and teased. Finally, he is chained between two pillars which hold up their palace, and, as there are three thousand of his enemies in attendance, he asks the Lord to grant him one last grace: vengeance in exchange for his life. As described in Judges 16, the prayer is granted, and Samson, in a triumphal expression of superhuman strength, pulls down the pillars of the Philistine palace, causing the roof to collapse, killing everyone, including himself. For many Rastafarians, the lesson here is that a man must remain true to his roots— hair and spirit entwined—and watch out for the wicked.

The Rastafarian use of Samson as a figure of living folk-lore comes from the insistence that hair is a kind of talisman; regard the 60s habit among Rastas of "flashing locks," throwing the head from side to side and sending the arrow-like cords in all directions. Bob Marley says in the song "Rastamon Live Up":

> Keep your culture
> Don't be afraid of the vulture
> Grow your dreadlocks
> Don't be afraid of the wolf pack.

And:

> David slew Goliath
> With a single stone
> Samson slew the Philistines
> With a donkey jawbone.

There is a Rasta version of the story of Samson, told in this instance by a Jamaican rootsman, a bush doctor, living in the Parish of St. Mary.

The storyteller's name is Morris Oliphant and he says that he has an uncle, a man who is very strong. "My uncle's name is Samson, and he is very big. No one would ever think of stealing from Samson, and the people in his village feel protected just having him around. However, once a month Samson would count the money that he had earned; and this was the one time when he took certain precautions. He kept a machete on the table while he counted the coins and paper money that he had collected from his work that month.

"As I say, Samson is a very big, a very thick man. He had no real worries about anyone stealing from him, but one day he had gotten his locks caught in a threshing machine and had to cut some of them off. Because of this, he felt vulnerable.

"That night, three thieves came up to Samson's house, and they peeked into his open window. They saw him in the lantern light, counting his currency and coin. Of course, they also saw his size and his machete. But they took no alarm at this, since they were three, and he was one.

"Now, Samson could lift a fieldplow by the handle and hold it out before him with one hand. He could squat underneath a donkey and raise the animal into the air on his shoulders, so that the donkey's legs dangled. He was very strong, Samson. But no man, no matter how powerful, is invulnerable. One of the thieves carried a pistol; the other two had ratchet knives. So now they walked into the open doorway and the three stood in the light so that they could be plainly seen.

"The first thief pointed his gun at Samson, and told him not to move or he would shoot him. Then he ordered the other two to go to the table and take up the money that was lying there. Samson, seeing the men approach, acted quickly. He threw a handful of coins in the face of one and the second he chopped with his machete. Then he overturned the table and snuffed out the light. The pistol man fired two shots into the darkness. One of the bullets nicked Samson's ear; another passed harmlessly through the palm of his right hand.

"Well, the thief who'd been struck by the coins dove on top of Samson while his partner writhed on the floor, suffering a machete cut across the chest. The pistol man waited for just the right moment to stick his gun into Samson's mouth. Samson knew it was too late to do anything but shut his eyes, which he did, just as the gun went off with a roar that lit up the room. The bullet jerked open Samson's mouth, and bore a hole in his cheek.

"Now Samson brought up his knee, jamming the pistol man in the groin. Samson started to crawl across the floor to get away, but his adversary fired another shot, and this time Samson felt a sting on his right buttock.

"Then there was a click as one of the thieves whipped out a ratchet knife. Samson heard the click of the open blade, and he swept the floor with his leg. There was a loud whack as the knife-wielding man's feet went wheeling out from under him, and he hit the back of his head on the concrete floor. That left but one—the pistoleer—but he was doubled-up, and before he could recover, Samson picked up the table and dropped it on him.

"All in all, Samson came out all right in the scuffle. The bullet that went into his mouth ripped out a rotten molar that had been troubling him for months, and the bullet that went into his backside took care of a sciatic problem he'd had for years. After this, Samson didn't count his money anymore, for, as he vowed: 'Keep no lock on your money, but just on your head.'"

WISDOM

I Now the whole kingdom of the world belonged to the seed of Shem, the seed of Abram, the seed of David, the seed of Solomon. The Father gave glory to the seed of Shem because of the blessing he bestowed upon Noah. Solomon himself was the wisest king who ever lived; his wisdom and his understanding were immeasurable.

Solomon lived by his word, and the readiness of his mouth was balanced by the discretion of his speech, and his life spoke in his behalf, so that his sitting down and rising up, his table and his law, his work, his love, and his life were all one. Those to whom he gave orders felt that his words were kind and those who committed faults were admonished gently. Solomon's house was built upon the wisdom of the Father, and Solomon smiled graciously on fools and to the wise he said parables that had the sweetness of honey.

II Now when the Queen of the South, Makeda, heard of him, she wished to know more about him. And it happened that a leader of the Queen's merchant caravan came to King Solomon's palace. There he learned that Solomon was building a great tabernacle to offer praise to the Father. In exchange for certain goods which he needed for building the temple, Solomon gave silver and gold; and the merchant leader, whose name was Tamrin, heard of this and came to see him.

And Tamrin was told by Solomon to bring whatsoever he wished from the country of Arabia; red, gold, and black wood that could not be eaten by worms and sapphires that burned like the fires of heaven. So Tamrin saw that Solomon was not just a king, but also a great man. Moreover, he noticed that the Father had provided him with abundance, so that gold was as common as bronze and silver was as common as lead, and that each was as plentiful as the grass of the field.

So Tamrin the merchant left the country of Judah and Jerusalem and returned to Ethiopia to meet his queen, and there told her what he had heard and seen. And he told her that there was nothing false about Solomon and that everything he ac-complished was the handicraft of his vision and the perfection of his wisdom. Tamrin spoke about the people who lived under Solomon's rule, saying how no man defrauded another, and how no man stole from his neighbor, and how there was neither thief nor robber among them, but the people lived in peace.

III Now each morning the Queen asked Tamrin again what he might recall of Solomon and his kingdom, for she wanted very much to see all of this for herself, and yet she was afraid because the journey was a long and arduous one. Tamrin repeated, always, the same great things: that in the country of Solomon there was no imperfection. Thus did her heart incline to go; and thus did the Father put that longing there. So she prepared for the long journey because, as she spoke of it to her people, "I am smitten with love of wisdom."

And the Queen spoke of the power of wisdom, and her people paid heed to what she said. For, she explained, "Wisdom is far better than the treasure of silver and gold. It is sweeter than honey and finer than wine, brighter than the sun, and to be loved more than precious stones. What is stored within it is greater than oil, and it satisfies one's craving more than meat. It is joy to the heart, light to the eye, speed to the foot, and shield to the breast.

"Wisdom is the best of all treasures. He who stores gold has no profit without wisdom, and he who stores wisdom—no man can steal it away." Then the Queen made ready to set out on her journey. Seven hundred and ninety-seven camels were loaded and mules and asses too, and she set out on her journey and followed the road,

and her heart was given confidence by the Father.

IV And she arrived in Jerusalem bringing many precious gifts to the King. He gave her a place to stay in the royal palace near him and sent her food morning and night, gazelles and fatted fowls and measures of old wine. He sent singing men and women, fine honey, and rich sweets. Every day he arrayed her in garments that bewitched the eye. And all the while Solomon was working at the building of the House of the Father. Everything was wrought by his order and there was no opposition to his word; for the light of his heart was like a lamp in the darkness, and his words of wisdom were as abundant as the sand grains of the desert. And the speech of beasts and birds was not hidden from him, and he did everything by means of the skill which the Father had given him. He did not ask for victory over his enemy, nor for riches or fame. Solomon only asked for wisdom whereby he might rule his people and build the Father's House.

And the Queen Makeda spoke to King Solomon: "I look upon you and see that your wisdom is immeasurable and your understanding inexhaustible. These are like a pomegranate in the garden, a pearl in the sea, and the morning star at dawn. I give thanks to Our King and Our Creator, who brought me here so that I might hear your voice."

V And King Solomon answered Queen Makeda: "Wisdom and understanding spring from your heart, too. As for me, I have them only because the Father of Israel has given them to me and because I asked him for them. I do not serve according to my own will but according to the Father's. My speech springs not from myself but it is only what the Father makes me utter. Whatsoever he commands me to do, I do. Wheresoever he wishes me to go, I go. Whatsoever he teaches me, I speak. For once I was dust and now I am flesh; once I was water and now I am solid; for the Father fashioned me in his own likeness, and made me in his own image."

As Solomon was talking with the Queen, he saw a laborer walk by them. The man had a stone upon his head, a skin of water upon his neck, and his sandals were tied about his loins. The man carried pieces of wood in his hands and the sweat fell in drops from his face and wetted his ragged clothing. And the laborer passed before Solomon and the King said unto him, "Stand still." And the laborer stood.

Then the King turned to the Queen and said, "Look at this man. Am I superior to him? In what way am I better? How shall I glory over him? I am a man of dust and ash who will soon become worms, and yet at this moment I appear like one who would never die. Both of us are beings, that is to say, men. His death is my death; and his life is my life. Yet this man is stronger as a worker than I am. For the Father has given power to those as it pleases Him to do." Then Solomon said to the laborer, "Go to your work now."

VI Solomon then said to the Queen, "Of what use are we, the children of men, if we do not use kindness and love? Are we not grass upon the field, which withers in its season and is burnt by fire? We wear fine clothes and eat excellent food and we bathe our-selves in sweet scent, and yet, being wise, we are still fools. The man made in the image of the Father should become like Him. Let the arrogant and the honorless be judged along with the Devil. For the Father loves the humble, and those who practice humility walk in the way of the Father and rejoice in His Kingdom. Blessed is the man who knows wisdom, which is to say compassion, which is to say love of the Father."

Then Queen Makeda said to Solomon, "How greatly your words please me. Tell me now: Whom shall I worship? We worship the sun as our fathers have taught us. We worship the sun because he cooks our food and he lightens the darkness. We call him Our King, Our Creator, we worship him as a god, for no man has told us that there is another. But now we hear that there is with you, Israel, another god, whom we do not know. Men have told us that He sent you a Tabernacle and a Tablet, ordered by angels and delivered by the hand of Moses. This we have heard and that He, Himself, has come down to you and has talked to you, giving you His Commandments."

Rastas have created an oral mythology around the use of marijuana, ganja, weed, herb. The myths that are associated with the smoking of marijuana come from splinters of psalms in the Bible and from Ethiopian tales that go back to Solomon's time as king. One of these suggests that ganja plants sprang out of Solomon's grave after he was buried. There are aphorisms that state that "to smoke renders one as wise as Solomon" or that "herb is the wine," the blessing of sacrament, the advocation of the Lord.

The myth of the tree of wisdom is intertwined with many other myths in Jamaica, so many that it is almost impossible to trace them, to determine where they begin or end, or where they come back around and start again. However, this, too, is like the tree itself.

The wild fig tree which grows all over Jamaica is a great iron-trunked tree with clasping roots descending deep into the earth, making caves of the rock substructure below it. One day, a Rastaman named Roy tells a great story about the Tree of Life.

"A farmer that I knew had a great fig tree growing on his land, and beneath it there was a fresh water spring. Well, he thought the tree was getting too much water to drink, so he chopped it down, and immediately the spring dried up; and then all of the trees on his farm began to die because he had no water to give them. So, then, he took a small cutting of the original fig tree, and he planted it in a good place, but not the same one where the first spring had been. And every day he said prayers over the little cutting. And he blew a fresh breath of the smoke of the herb on the small planting, and he prayed for its deliverance and his own, for his farm was withering in the sun. And the tree grew and prospered and drew water unto it and the water made a cleft in the earth, and that cleft became a spring, which nourished the tree; and once again there was water on that farmer's land."

Roy pauses a moment to light a spliff. He blows some smoke in the direction of the tree on the hill overlooking his land. He says that this is the "natural mystic" blowing through the air, the sacred smoke of the Tree of Life.

"For the Father did say, 'Let the earth bring forth grass, and herb yielding seed, and the fruit tree yielding fruit after his kind, whose seed is itself, after his kind.'"

"So the sacred herb of the Rastaman," I tell him, "is also the Tree of Life in the Bible."

Roy brushes my knuckles with his, and adds, "It is the Tree of Wisdom, for, if you have wisdom, then you have life. Fools suffer from want of wisdom; fools die from lack of knowledge. It is written. But if herb made Solomon wise, then surely the power of the Father was proven, and put to good use on earth for all of us."

Later we take a ride through Walker's Wood and up Fern Gulley, and over the hill to Moneague, and back up into the birth country of Bob Marley, the town called Nine Miles. Everyone here calls it Nine Mile, conveniently dropping the plural, for conversational ease.

Everything about the ride is redolent of a pilgrimage, a journey into the biblical backwoods. The minibus we're riding in is dubbed Irie One, which in patois means "happy one." The bus itself is packed full of old country Rastas, and one of them, Selvin Johnson, works at Tuff Gong in Kingston, and was a follower of Bob Marley during the 70s. He remembers those days well and there is a lot which he can, and, of course, cannot, talk about. Bob Marley is more than a man to Selvin; he is a prophet.

In her essay "Journey to Nine Miles," Alice Walker observed that Nine Miles is "one of the stillest and most isolated spots on the face of the earth." As the bus creaks over the marl roads and we stare out at the twisted acacia trees, the great-trunked guangos, clustered with blooming air plants, the green hills whose reddish burnt soil pushes out white boney rocks that stick out like ribs. We do, indeed, seem to be nearing some kind of lost paradise.

I watch the fig trees as we roll by; they are rooted in the rocks. And the playing fields of the Lord stretch out on all sides of us as small boys riding a donkey and driving goats wave to us as we pass through this red earth, rolling turf, a dreamland of palm copses and distant houses made of wattle and daub.

I see the switches in their hands, and the little girls waving bunches of guineps, and the road goes steadily, grindingly upward.

I am reminded of the fact that Bob Marley came of country stock, the son of a white English soldier by the name of Norval Marley and a black Jamaican woman named Cedella Booker. It was she who came from this lovely scriptural land, where Bob spent much of his boyhood, learning the lore of bush and Bible from his grandfather, Omeriah, who was, from all accounts, a mystic man.

"My songs have a message of righteousness," Bob Marley once explained, "whether you're black . . . listen, man, you know I am not prejudice about myself. Because my father's white, my mother's black. You know what them call me, half-caste or whatever." He also said that the God who made him made "technicolor people," and he said, "I am nothing. All I have is God."

Once he denied the name Bob Marley, saying that he did not know his rightful name yet, but this was not important to him. The only thing that mattered to Bob Marley, the artist, was helping people: "My head is not in the material world. I am a man who sleeps on stone. Go into the hills and rest. That's my pleasure. I own the earth, you know, all things belong to I."

When we finally arrive at Nine Mile, a Rasta offers us herb at the store at the foot of the hill that leads up to the stained-glass windowed mausoleum where Bob Marley is buried. He says, "You should blow some smoke on the spot where Bob's resting." We buy a brown paper sack full of sweet heathery-smelling weed, and that which topples out of the bag during the transaction is swept aside by the bare, leathery foot of the herbsman. Off the porch it goes, perhaps a hundred U.S. dollars' worth. He notices my dismay.

"No worry," he intones, "there's plenty more of that." Then he laughs and the other Rastas on the veranda laugh with him. And then we walk, the group of us, up the hill to a place of burnt offerings.

I hold in my hand a bag of natural mystic—what Bob once called *kaya,* which is the name for the old-fashioned, coconut-fiber stuffing used in Jamaican bedding. I have slept on kaya beds before, and they give the best country sleep imaginable.

Within the compound we walk around, breathing the clear air of Marley's birthplace. Selvin takes me to the "rock-stone" that Bob sang about in "Talking Blues."

> Cold ground was my bed last night
> And rock was my pillow, too
> I have been down on the rock so long
> I seem to wear a permanent screw

"Here he would come to rest," Selvin says, "to meditate, to stare at Jah's reflection in the sky at all hours of the night. And here, too, Ziggy come and do the same thing. Look, you come rest your body on the dirt and the stone that Bob lay on, and feel what he felt when he rest his spirit here."

We make our way over to the south side of the mausoleum where the others are burning herb.

"Why did Bob have to die so young?" I ask Selvin.

Selvin draws some smoke, offers some to me. I accept and pass it back to Selvin, who says, "You see, Bob was carrying a lot of weight. Maybe too much weight. You know, he say, 'Every man think his burden the heaviest.' And so it become, even unto Bob."

The Jamaican John Crows, turkey vultures, swoop low, making their slow circles, dropping down to rest on a bare tree not far from the gravesite. "They always go to where there is a dead," Roy observes.

"No dead bury here," Selvin states.

Then, he adds, "No black man could hold up the weight Bob had on his back: for he was carrying the whole world. A killing weight, that. But no matter, for he is with us now. Look into Ziggy's eyes, you see Bob. Listen to him sing, you hear Bob. And in Steve, and Kymani, and Cedella, and all of the youth them: Bob live. Understand?"

The herb of the tree of life keeps making its rounds, keeps going round and refreshing us, as the breeze off the hills of Nine Mile returns.

The blue smoke trails out in the wind that moves the branches of the ganja trees whose roots grow strong into the earth of Bob's final resting place.

Selvin says, "The herb of wisdom grew out of King Solomon's grave, and as Bob did say, 'Some are roots, some are branches. I and I are the roots.' "

Rastafarians are patriarchal. Jamaican society is itself patterned in some respects after the old African manner of male chiefdom and secondary wives. Yet, as evidenced by our years in Jamaica, the woman, without question, rules. It is she who is ultimately responsible, it seems, for everything domestic. And that includes all except politics. The Kebra Nagast is usually blind when it comes to the presence of women (including the excision of Eve in the first section), but the portrait of Makeda, the Queen of the South, is exceptional for its comparison with Solomon. While subservient to him in wisdom, at first, she matches him in courage. Later, she incorporates and surpasses his wisdom—she, in fact, does not have a "falling out" with the Father. And, as a woman in a man's world, she rivals him in power. It should be remembered that her reign was first sponsored by an event of nature's own making. Prior to Makeda's, or Sheba's, queenship, she was a simple tribal woman, but there was something that set her apart. To her befell the opportunity to become a mystic ruler, one who had been chosen by some force of nature. The following tale, as told by a member of the Ethiopian Orthodox Church, was given to him by elders in the church. When he told it, his words were almost identical with the Kebra Nagast.

Sheldon is a "sealed" locksman, one who has formally joined the Ethiopian Orthodox Church. He is well read, well spoken, and confident. He often speaks about the Tree of Life in Genesis and how that tree is the same one that blessed Solomon.

"The Tree of Life is anything that bears the fruit of which we partake and live. But as David, the prophet, declared, 'God Reigneth in the wood.' What that means is that the Queen of Sheba was blessed by the wood of the tree of Paradise, and that it healed her cloven foot.

"It was a devil thing, a magic worked by the devil. She was a pretty Abyssinian girl. One day, she was walking when she saw a dragon coming towards her and she hid in the branches of a tree. Now this same dragon was seen and executed by some holy men, some Ethiopian saints. Just as the creature died, a drop of dragon's blood spotted the foot of that girl. And her foot, the one struck by that blood, turned into a cloven hoof. Now when she returned to her village, it became known that the dragon was dead. So the people honored the girl for killing it, even though she hadn't, and they made her their queen. And that is how she came to be known as the Queen of Sheba, which was the country of her birth."

Sheldon returns to the story of Sheba's foot.

"Solomon the King would not permit such ungodliness to pass before his eyes. He healed her himself. It is in the Kebra Nagast. When she stepped over the threshold of his palace, she was miraculously healed. Just like that! To understand this, we must go back to when Solomon was first building his palace. He could find no stonemasons whose art would cut through the giant blocks of stone. So he sent some of his workers into the mountains and they captured a young eagle there, as he had instructed them. This bird was placed by Solomon under a brass pot, yet the wings were so large they poked out from under the pot. Now the mother eagle, seeing her young one thus caught up, flew over to Eden and took from a tree there a piece of wood, which she carried back to Solomon's courtyard. Dropping the wood from the air, she passed over the brass pot that almost, but not quite, concealed her offspring.

"Now, that small piece of wood, when it struck the pot that held the bird captive, broke apart. The mother eagle then claimed what was hers, her child. But she left the wood where it had broken the pot and she returned with her young to the nest. And that wood is the very thing that King Solomon gave to his head stonemason to build his palace and shelter the Ark of the Covenant. That wood was sacred, a gift of God. When the mason put it upon the most obdurate stone, the rock gave way, as if cleaved by the Father Himself. This was the wood, too, in the threshold that Sheba crossed over. And so it is, and so it shall ever be in the name of the Most High, Selassie I, King of Kings, Lord of Lords, Conquering Lion of the Tribe of Judah. Jah, Rastafari."

I The kingdom of Rome was the dominion of Japheth, the son of Noah. Of those generations which were eighteen from the days of Darius to the days of Solomon, there was born a man whose name was Zanbares. A seer and a stargazer, he foresaw what would come: that the kingdom would depart from the children of Japheth and would come to the seed of David, of the tribe of Shem. And when he saw this he sent a message to David the King, which said, "Take my daughter for your son." So Solomon had a son by her and called his name Adrami. And Zanbares died and Balthazar, one of his kinsmen, became king. But he lacked a child to reign after him and he asked Solomon the King to provide him with a son who would become King of Rome. For as he said, "I have but three daughters and no male children. And I will give whichever of my daughters pleases your son; and he shall have the throne and the city of Rome."

Solomon therefore vowed to send him Adrami, his youngest son. And Balthazar rejoiced and gave Adrami his eldest daughter, whose name was Adlonya. Now one day Balthazar wished to test the son of Solomon to see whether he truly possessed his father's wisdom. Therefore he gave before him a trial concerning the owner of a vineyard and a shepherd whose flock of sheep had spoiled it.

The shepherd asked to have his sheep returned to him, and he said that the vineyard owner had carried them off. So Adrami listened to the other man's appeal, the grower of grapes.

"How much of the vineyard have the sheep eaten?" Adrami asked. "Have they devoured the leaves or the tendrils? Have they consumed the young grapes or the roots of the shoots?"

And the owner of the vineyard answered and said, "They have eaten the tendrils and the branches that have grapes upon them. There is nothing left of the vines except the twigs."

"Is this true?" Adrami asked the shepherd.

"My lord, the sheep ate only the tendrils with leaves on them."

Adrami questioned, "But the grower has just said your sheep ate the grapes, and all but the twigs close to the very root."

The shepherd said, "No, my lord, they ate the blossoms before they had turned into grapes."

Now Adrami gave his judgment to the grower of grapes. "Listen to what I say now. If the sheep have eaten all the shoots from the root of the vine, then all the sheep belong to you. But if they have eaten the leaves of the branches and the blossoms thereon, then you shall take the sheep and shear their wool. You may also take the young of those which have not yet given birth. As for the sheep which have already had their young, leave these to the shepherd, for they shall be his."

When Balthazar heard of the judgment he said, "This is a judgment of the people of the God of Israel. For everything works according to its own season and the temper of its time. Therefore, wage war with one who would wage war, rule him that would be ruled, keep alive him that should be kept alive, and judge fairly or not at all."

Soon after this a fever took hold of Balthazar, and after he died, Adrami ruled the kingdom. And the city of Rome became his possession; and of the generations that came after him, it was also theirs by the will of God.

ANGEL

I It came to pass that there was a man of the seed of Shem named Karmin. He lived in Manasseh under the King of Israel. Karmin was good in all ways and there was no evil whatsoever in him. He was rich in camels and horses, flocks of sheep and herds of cattle. He had gold, silver, and fine apparel. Now it happened that his native country was Judah but he lived in Israel and those who lived around him were envious of his wealth. There were those who wished to drive him away from their country. There was a deceitful man of the seed of Benjamin whose name was Benyas. Benyas went to his lord, the King Manasseh, and told him that Karmin spoke against him

and his country. The King said, "Is there any man who has heard of this other than yourself?" And Benyas said he would produce witnesses. And this he did though these men lied with the same intent as Benyas. Therefore the King's decision was to kill Karmin and confiscate all of his possessions: his pastures and wells, his flocks and herds, his gold and silver.

Then Benyas went to Karmin and befriended him and achieved his confidence; and Karmin had no idea that Benyas and his companions who ate and drank in his own household were his worst enemies. Then was fulfilled the prophecy of King David, who said, "Those who speak words of peace with their neighbor and hold evil in their hearts are rewarded according to the evil of their works and the evil of their thoughts."

So these men ate and drank and became drunk in the house of Karmin, and they slept as one of the family in the beds that were provided. But after they had fallen asleep an Angel of God awoke Karmin and said, "Leave your possessions and save yourself, for these men are traitors and the King has ordered your death sentence."

And Karmin rose up straight away and taking as much treasure as he could carry went forth in the night with his wife and children. His wife and sons he sent with two servants to go to Jerusalem, while he himself departed to a remote country, a distance of three months' journey, called Babylon.

And Benyas and his evil companions who had borne lying testimony were killed in bed in Karmin's house by the soldiers of the King of Israel.

I In Babylon Karmin was welcomed by the King and given a place to stay in the house of his merchant who was away for three years. Karmin seduced the wife of the merchant, who soon became heavy with child. And the woman wished to throw the child whom she had conceived into the river for she feared the merchant, her husband.

And at that time the wife of the King of Babylon also conceived and brought forth a child which resembled an eaglet without wings. So she called a handmaiden to send the thing away in a wicker basket, and to cast the creature into the river without telling anyone about it. And in the same night the merchant's wife sent her handmaiden also to the river.

And by the will of God both handmaidens met at the river, and they talked together. The Queen's handmaiden said, "My lady has brought forth a child which has not the appearance of a man, but of a wingless eagle, and she has commanded me to throw it into the river." But the handmaiden of the merchant's wife said that her mistress had given her a fine son which she was to dispose of in a similar manner. So the two women made an agreement, and the Queen's handmaiden took the good son of the merchant's wife. And the other woman accepted the bird, which she then cast into the river.

II And it was reported to the King that the Queen had borne a son. The Queen gave the boy to the nurses and he grew up in the house of the King. And she called him Nebuchadnezzar, which means "by the luck of the bird." And he became the King of Babylon, and through Karmin he was of the seed of Shem. And in time he became King, and overthrew Jerusalem, and carried away the children of Israel. And they wandered in the town of Babylon with the grandchildren of Manasseh, the king of Israel.

Nebuchadnezzar was so rich that he set up a pillar of gold on the plain of Babylon. He boasted, "I make the sun shine in the heavens." Moreover, he worshiped idols. But God punished him severely so that he might know the truth, and Nebuchadnezzar knew the name of the Lord and He had compassion upon him and brought him back to the Kingdom of Babylon, where he stayed and where his seed was passed on forever.

Hawks, angels, and babes in baskets may seem to be images of a disparate nature, but in the Kebra Nagast they are related to some very old Babylonian myths, and some of these have survived in the Bible and also into Western (Greek and Roman) mythology. The core teaching in the Kebra Nagast is that we must learn to live by the law of compassion rather than judgment. We must also learn to embrace the encumbrances that would seek, we think, to pull us down and vanquish us. Luck, according to Rastas, is not a wish granted by fate, but part of the fabric of "livity," or life lived to the fullest extent of compassion. Thus, to the unjudging eye, do hawks sometimes resemble angels floating across the heavens. And so, too, can babes in swaddling clothes resemble, not monsters, but monstrous situations, which are often overcome.

In Jamaica the smallest of raptors, the kestrels, are called killy hawks. The name comes from the cry that accompanies their dive, the sudden swerve and drop on the unwary. That cry of victory over the blind, the newly born, the just taken is unmistakable. A chilling cry it is, a high scrapy song.

Benji walks up Firefly Hill with me and we hear the killy hawks crying, shrilling overhead. They hover, light as the air on the coastal thermals, their wings outspread like tiny paper kites as they swoop up on the uplift of the draft. Up we climb among the tribes of tethered goats.

We are hot, sweat faced. Jewels sparkle on Benji's brow. We stop for a moment to rest.

"Was that your son I saw today?" I ask Benji.

He says, proudly, "I raised that boy, you know. I had no help from his mother."

We have caught our breath now, and we begin to move up towards the top of the hill.

Benji pays the bowstring song of the hawks no mind; he keeps climbing, until we walk at last along a quiet goat path at the summit of the mountain, and he spies a sour orange tree.

"I used to work up here making charcoal," Benji explains after the long interval of quiet. "That was before the coming of my boy. The way it happened was like this. One night I awakened from a dream, and I heard the wailing of a baby. I went outside and, lying in the moonlight, I saw a babe in a basket. The baby-mother had put him there and gone on her way. So there was no use trying to find that woman who didn't want to be a mother. I found myself standing dazed in the moonlight, gazing at my child."

Benji walks over to the sour orange tree and plucks a bright fruit from the springy branch. With his pocketknife, he unscrolls the covering of the orange. Then he says, "What I was saying, here is this child, my child. And I haven't got enough money to feed myself. And not even a loaf of hard dough bread, or a tin of sweet milk in the house. So, of course, I bring the basket in, and the child starts to cry because he is so very hungry."

The orange is now free of its skin, the flesh glistening. Benji gives me a section. I take a bite, and spit it out. I have never tasted anything so sour in all my life. "That's awful," I tell him, "bitter as poison."

"No, mon." Benji chuckles. "That is the fruit of life.

"This little orange," he grins, "born bitter. But, if you squeeze it properly, and you put some sugar with it, and then you add some water. Well, let me tell you, that is a drink. And you are never thirsty after you have drunk of it."

I look at him doubtfully.

"It is true," he says. And he starts to laugh. "It is the bitter with the sweet that is so good to the taste.

"So as I was telling you, the baby had to eat; and I had to work. But I couldn't work because I had to care for the baby. It was just so. Sometimes life catch you like that, and make things very bitter for you."

He tosses what is left of the orange into the ferns that grow in clumps by the trail. The pulpy fruit thumps away into the ferny tangle. Benji looks back to me.

"I know Jah will provide," he says with certainty. "But, when I was younger, I didn't have the reasoning power that I have now. So I didn't know how my luck would turn. But when that morning of truth came I had no money, no job, no food. The child, my child, is crying and crying. I am so vexed I cannot pray any more. So I open the door and look to the sea. There I see a boat with three fishermen in it. The men are fishing but there is no space in the boat for another person. Out there on the sea, the waves are tall. Behind that boat, I see someone swimming. A little boy swimming along after the boat. I am wondering why the fishermen don't stop to pick up the boy in such a rough sea. But then I come to an understanding—and it is Jah who put this idea into my head. That little boy's job is to dive for the fish traps, bring them up from the bottom. He is diving in that rough, rough sea for fish traps, and raising them up, all heavy with saltwater, all by himself. Just a little boy, too. Maybe ten years old. But so strong. Sometimes the sea cover him. I wouldn't see him or the boat. Then they would both bounce back into my sight."

Benji pauses for a moment. "Do you see what I am saying? If such a boy could live on the sea, I knew that my son could live on the land. I come up here on this hill, that very morning. And I start to make a living making charcoal out of pimento trees. Right here, where we sit. This is where I get my start, right here on these cold, old embers. And that grown boy you see down in the yard, he is old enough now to take care of himself, but he doesn't remember the night that I remember, standing in the moonlight, looking into his helpless face, wondering what in the world I am going to do."

I ask Benji how he made charcoal with the child about.

"Well," he answers, "I just carry him on my back while I cut the tree and burn the wood and do my work. Up here in the bush, there is plenty to eat—bush food. My boy was raised on things like that: Chinee banana, star apple, guava, June plum, guinep. I roasted breadfruit on the same coals that I sold in the village. Yes, those times were bitter, but they were good times."

On the way back down the hill to the village, Benji tells me that he knew a man once who was down so low that he tried to take his life. He went out into the bush and wrapped a vine around his neck, and was all set to jump off a tree, when he saw a ripe banana. So he plucked the banana and ate it. Then he wrapped his neck with the vine and was preparing to make the leap, when he saw a starving man, eating the banana peel he had just cast away. The sight of a man eating a banana peel on all fours like a dog brought the fellow to his senses.

"There are no angels," Benji explains, as we come back into the bustling village of Port Maria. "Just man."

"What about Jah?" I ask.

"That is what is meant by I and I," he replies. "Man and Jah, together, in this flesh, in this moment. The only angel we'll ever need."

Faith and fire, conviction and flame—the symbolism of these are Rasta through and through, which is why lions with manes outspread like burning suns are common images of the Rasta brotherhood. And it was King Nebuchadnezzar, a member of the old order of pagan kings in the Bible and the Kebra Nagast, who faced the fact that the faithful threesome of Shadrach, Meshach, and Abednego had such absolute faith in God that they feared nothing, not even the fiery furnace of that famous Babylonian king. Rastas enjoy this parable because it utilizes three things of which their beliefs are cast: fate, faith, and fire. Those who know do not merely believe; they "overstand" and they have no fear. Knowledge, like wisdom, comes direct from the heart, and the heart was put there, the Rastas tell us, by none other than Jah. The African Nyabinghi ceremony that the Rastas have adopted as their own has elements in it that come from the myths of Revelation in the Bible. These myths speak of world's end, immolation, Jah's judgment. Only the righteous shall be saved, so it is written. The Kebra Nagast speaks of the Second Coming and explains that when the Savior appears again he will free all of the great prophets from the jail of sheol. In Jamaica it is known that facing Jah is a daily occurrence and that sometimes the weak of heart grow strong by contemplation of fire. Faith draws the sufferers into the very heart of the fire of judgment.

The myth of Shadrach, Meshach, and Abednego tells of the three men whom King Nebuchadnezzar commanded to be bound and cast into a furnace heated seven times "more than it was wont to be heated." The three were so devout that they rose out of the fire unscathed. Thus was Nebuchadnezzar, the mighty king of Babylon, humbled before three simple men of Jerusalem. So, although it might have been against his previous desire, now the king made obeisance to the God of Israel. What he had seen was enough; fire had no power over three humans. No head was singed. No scent of flame remained on their clothes. And yet Shadrach, Meshach, and Abednego had leaped, fully clothed and hatted, into the fiery furnace of King Nebuchadnezzar. How did they do it? Through faith. Faith in the Creator. The Father. Jah.

The story is told over and over in Jamaica. The Rastafarians know it, so do the neo-Revivalists, the Catholics, the Jews, the Syriac Christians, the Orthodox Ethiopians, the Pocomaniacs, the Kuminists, and all other known and unknown religious orders.

The Rastas are deeply committed to this idea of purgation by fire. The expression they often use, *Bloodfire,* is an exultation. Blood is the sacred element of life, and Fire is the cleanser of blood.

Bloodfire implies the apocalypse of Revelation, where this theme is very prevalent. Perdition comes with lightning, fire from heaven. As it says in the scripture, so that "every island fled away, and the mountains were not found" (Revelation

16:20). Rasta cosmology grants many metaphors. *Island* may be a metaphor for the earth, but to Rastas it is also a literal tribute to the island of Jamaica. And the mountain of imprisonment, in this case, is the place the slaves were brought to. Some Rastafarians think this is the biblical prophecy as mentioned in Revelation.

Furthermore, in Revelation 17:5 we find this proclamation: "MYSTERY, BABYLON THE GREAT, THE MOTHER OF HARLOTS AND ABOMINATIONS OF THE EARTH." This, the Rastas say, is the world of wretched cities into which the poor Ethiopian is cast, not unlike Shadrach, Meshach, and Abednego, to come forth, unscathed by flame. To come out pure. To have the faith to be untouched by the blasphemy of the world's wrongdoing.

Tonight, we are traveling on the Junction, as it is called, that old, snaky slave road leading out of Kingston, crossing the Blue Mountains, and heading into the countryside. Here, at night, the tree frogs sing and the bamboo lamps burn, and wherever you look, men and women move on secret missions, carrying water on their heads, staring into the headlight glare as if our bus were the seven-faced beast of Babylon.

This night, as it happens, is the 104th birthday of Emperor Haile Selassie. Chin, a Chinese Rastafarian, has just returned from a Nyabinghi ceremony where a brethren jumped into the binghi fire and died.

He explains how it happened.

"The judgment fire had been burning since the twenty-third of July, and it would keep burning until the binghi was over, around the fourth of August. A brethren named Ike was standing near the fire when suddenly he jumped into the flames. Someone pulled him out right away, but in a little while, he jumped back in again, held onto one of the tree stumps in the heart of the fire, and wouldn't let go. The second time we stood there and watched him burn, his face melting like candle wax. It was as if he were screaming but no sound came out of his mouth, so it was like a silent scream, which no one could hear but Jah. Then, after that, his mouth seemed to close and he uttered baby noises like ooh and ahh, and then he shrank down to a small little size man about half what he was, and that was the end of him.

"I tried to save him," he says, "we all did. But it seems as if he had his mind made up to die that way and even when his locks fried out in that heat, he took it unto himself, for it was a thing between him and Jah. Fire, we know, is judgment. The first came with water, the second will come as fire; we know that. That is why the fire key is the presence of the Almighty and the judgment to come. But Ras Ike seemed to have felt this was his time, his judgment.

"I have seen the fire key some twenty-seven years now, and never saw anything like this. I mean, this man had a work to do and he did it, and no one could stop him. You have your road and you have to know your way. Ike took the road he knew he had to take. It is like that for all of us, and for all of us a judgment time will come."

We are almost home. I watch the wind punishing the

sugar cane. It is beautiful in the moonlight the way the cane, bending forward and away from the stem, shines as it is manipulated by the wind.

"You see the wind," Chin says. "It, too, is moved by the hand of the Father. And the sugar cane is a plaything of the wind, as well. But if we have a hurricane like Gilbert again, that same wind will turn fool. It will break the cane, destroy it like judgment. Jah judgment."

VISION

I Solomon said: "It is right that men should worship the Father, for he created the Universe, Heaven and Earth, He created the sea, the dry land, the sun, the moon, and the stars. He made the trees and the stones, the beast and the fowl, the crocodile and the fish. He made the whale and the hippopotamus, the water lizard and the gazelle. Therefore, it is right that we should worship Him with gladness, for the Father is the Lord of the universe, the maker of angels and men. It is He who punishes and He who shows compassion; it is He who exalts and He who condemns; it is He who raises up and He who brings down. And who among us can say to Him, What have you done?"

And Queen Makeda said, "From this time forward I shall no longer worship the sun. But I shall worship the creator of the sun, the God of Israel." And so it was that the Queen went to Solomon and he answered the questions which she put to him. But after she had dwelt there six months, the Queen wished to return to her own country. So she sent a message to Solomon: "I greatly wish to stay with you, but now, for the sake of my people, I must return to my own country. As for that which I have heard, let the Father make it bear fruit in my heart, and in the hearts of all those who will hear it from me."

II And King Solomon sent a message to the Queen:

"Will you go away without seeing the Kingdom and without dining with me?" And the Queen replied, "From being a fool I have become wise listening to your wisdom. Therefore, I shall stay according to your desire." Then Solomon had his palace prepared and the royal table set according to the law of his Kingdom. The Queen came and she was struck with wonder at the splendor of that which she saw. There were purple hangings and carpets and marble and precious stones, and everywhere there burned aromatic powders and the scent of myrrh, cassia, and frankincense came from all directions.

And Solomon sent meats to her chamber which would make her thirsty. And drinks mingled with vinegar and other dishes spiced with pepper. After the meal, the King rose up and went to the Queen and they were alone together. He said to her, "Take your ease here for love's sake until daybreak." And she said to him, "Swear to the God of Israel that you will not take me by force." And Solomon answered, "I swear that I will not, but you must swear to me that you will not take, by force, any of my possessions."

The Queen laughed at hearing this, and replied, "I have no need of your things, for as you know I am also very wealthy. Nonetheless I swear that I will not take any of your possessions." And he swore to her and made her swear to him. The King went up on his bed on one side of the chamber. Servants made ready her bed on the other side. And Solomon said to a young manservant, "Wash out the bowl and set in it a vessel of water while the Queen is looking on, then shut the doors and leave us in peace."

III Now the King pretended to be asleep, but he was really watching the Queen. For her part, she slept for a little while and woke, dry with thirst. The food had made her very thirsty. Now she looked at King Solomon, and watched him carefully. At last she decided he was asleep. But he was not asleep, he was waiting until she should rise up to steal the water that was put between them.

So the Queen rose up and went to the water in the bowl and lifted the jar to drink. Yet Solomon seized her hand before she could drink and said, "Why have you already broken your oath that you would not take, by force, anything in my house?"

"Is the oath broken by my drinking water?"

"Is there anything under heaven richer than water?"

"Then I have sinned against myself, and you are free of your oath," she told him.

"I am free from the oath which you made me swear?"

"Yes, but please let me drink your water."

So Solomon permitted her to drink and after she had drunk her fill, they made love and then slept together.

IV After he slept, there appeared to King Solomon a dazzling vision. He saw a brilliant Sun come down from heaven and shed great splendor over Israel. There it stayed for a time, but suddenly withdrew itself and flew away to the country of Ethiopia, where it shone brightly forever. Solomon waited to see if the brilliance would come back to Israel but it did not return. Then, while he waited, a light rose up in the heavens and another Sun came down in the country of Judah, and it sent forth light which was much stronger than before.

Now Israel, because of the flame of that Sun, refused to walk in the light thereof. And that Sun paid no heed to Israel and the Israelites hated Him, and it became impossible that peace should exist between them and the Sun. And they raised their hands against Him with staves and knives, and they wished to extinguish that Sun. Thus they cast darkness upon the whole world. And earthquakes came and thick darkness. They had destroyed His light and they set a guard over His tomb wherein they had cast Him. And He came forth where they did not look for Him, and illumined the whole world. Those places most bathed in His light were the First Sea, the Last Sea, Ethiopia, and Rom. And He paid no heed, no heed whatsoever to Israel, and he ascended his former throne.

When Solomon the King saw this vision he became disturbed. His understanding went away and he woke with a troubled mind.

The Queen said to Solomon, "Let me depart to my own country." Solomon gave her camels and wagons and had them laden with beautiful things. He also gave her a vessel wherein one could traverse the sea, and a vessel wherein one could traverse the wind—these Solomon made by the wisdom which God gave him.

I Solomon then took the Queen aside and he removed the ring that was on his little finger, and he gave it to the Queen. "Take this so that you will not forget me. And if you should become pregnant, let this ring be his or her sign. And if a man-child should come to me, the peace of the Father will be with you. Now while I was sleeping, I saw many visions in a dream. The sun rose upon Israel, but it went away and lighted up the country of Ethiopia. So that country shall be blessed through you. The Father knows this to be true. And as for you, you may worship Him with all your heart and perform His will. For everything is His and none can oppose His judgment in the heavens or in the earth, the sea, the abysses. Go in peace."

Nine months and five days from the time the Queen had separated from King Solomon, she came into the country of Baa Zadisareya. There she brought forth a man-child, and then came to her own country, where there was a great welcoming.

II The child grew and she called him Bayna-Lehkem. When the child reached the age of twelve, he asked his friends who his father was. And they answered, "Solomon the King." So he went to the Queen, his mother, and said, "I wish to know my father." And the Queen said, "I am your father and your mother. You may seek no further." Yet the boy asked about his father often, so one day she told him, "Your father's country is far away and the road is rough. Wouldn't you rather be here?" The boy, who handsomely resembled his father, waited until he was twenty-two years old, and then he said to the Queen, "I will go and look upon the face of my father. And then I will come back here, by the will of the God, the Lord of Israel." Then the Queen took the young man aside and she gave him the ring so that the father might know his son, and the Queen sent Bayna-Lehkem away in peace.

And the young man journeyed until he came into the neighborhood of Gaza, the same country which Solomon gave to the Queen. And when the young man arrived in his mother's country, he was honored, for the people thought him to be the perfect likeness of Solomon the King. The people of Gaza said, "This is King Solomon." But there were some who said, "The King is in Jerusalem building his house." They argued with one another and they sent off spies to seek out King Solomon. And when the spies came to the watchmen of the city of Jerusalem, they found King Solomon there, and they said to him, "A merchant has come into our country who resembles you. His eyes are glad like a man who has drunk wine; his legs are strong; his neck is like David, your father."

III When King Solomon heard this, his heart was troubled but his soul was glad. For in those days he had no children known to him except for his seven-year-old boy named Rehoboam. Yet Solomon had once vowed, "By one thousand women I shall have one thousand men-children, and I shall inherit the countries of the enemy and I will overthrow their idols." But now a son that he did not know was at his gate. And this son would become King over the Tabernacle of the Law, Heavenly Zion, the King of Ethiopia.

Benaiah, the commander of the army of King Solomon, told Bayna-Lehkem that the country of the King was better than the country of his mother, the Queen. The commander said, "We have heard that your country is a land of cold and cloud, a country of heat glare and snow. This was the land given to Canaan, the son of Ham. And it is a land of whirlwind and sun, but the land that is ours is the promised land, a land of milk and honey. This country of ours is yours, for you are the seed of David, the Lord of my Lord."

A spokesman for Bayna-Lehkem replied, "Our country is good and it is without burning heat and fire. Sweet water flows in its rivers and the mountaintops run with freshets of water, and we do not need to dig deep wells. We do not suffer from the heat of the sun, but even at noonday we hunt the wild gazelle. In the winter the Father watches over us, and in the spring the people eat what grows from the soil, and their trees make good fruit and the wheat and barley are plentiful and the cattle are good and wonderful. Yet there is one thing that you have which is greater than ours: wisdom. Because of this we have come."

IV When Bayna-Lehkem came through the King's gate, the soldiers saw him and said, "Behold, King Solomon." And yet the King himself still sat upon his throne. And when

King Solomon saw his son he rose up and embraced him. And he kissed his mouth and forehead and eyes, and he said, "Behold my father David has renewed his youth and has risen from the dead." Then he said to all of his court, "You told me that he was my very image, but it is not so. He is David, my father, in the days of his early manhood, and he is more handsome than I."

And the men of the court answered, "Blessed be the mother who has brought forth this young man. And blessed be the day wherein you had union with the mother of this young man. For there has risen upon us from the grandfather of Solomon, whose name was Jesse, a shining man who shall be king of our posterity. Truly, he is an Israelite of the seed of David. Fashioned perfectly in the likeness of his father's form. We are his servants, and he shall be our king." Now the young man took the ring which his mother had given him and he said to his father, "Take this ring and remember the words you spoke to the Queen, and give us a portion of the fringe of the covering of the Tabernacle of the Law of God, so that we may worship it all of our days."

The King answered, "Why do you give me the ring as a sign? For even without it, I recognize that you are indeed my son."

And the merchant Tamrin spoke to King Solomon, and said, "The Queen, my mistress, said, 'Take this young man and make him King over our country, and give him the command that a woman shall never again reign in our land, and then send him back in peace.' "

I Solomon asked his son, "Why do you wish to depart from me? What do you lack here that you would go to the country of the heathen?" And his son answered, "I must go to my mother with your blessing, for you have a son who is better than I and whose name is Rehoboam, who was born of your lawful wife, while my mother is not your wife according to the law."

"Since you speak in this way," Solomon said, "you should know that I myself am not the son of my father David, who took the wife of another man whom he caused to be slain in battle, and he begot me by her. Yet the Father is compassionate and He has forgiven him. And who is more foolish than a man? And who is as compassionate and as wise as the Father?"

But no matter what Solomon said to his son, the young man remained unmoved. He said, "Oh, my Lord, it is impossible for me to leave the country of my mother, for I swore to her that I would soon return, and that I would not marry a wife. The Father of Israel shall bless me wherever I shall be, and your prayer shall accompany me wherever I go. I wanted to see your face and to hear your voice and to receive your blessing and now I desire to depart to my mother in safety."

II So Solomon gathered together his counselors and the elders of his kingdom and he said, "I am not able to make this young man consent to dwell here, so let us make him King of the country of Ethiopia. Together with your children, you sit on my right hand and on my left hand, and in like manner the eldest of your children should sit on his right hand and on his left hand. Let us give him your firstborn children and we shall have two kingdoms. I will rule here with you and our children shall reign there with him."

And so the counselors, officers, and elders made ready to provide their children and send them into the country of Ethiopia so that they might reign and dwell there forever, they and their seed from generation to generation.

So they made ready the oil of kingship. And the sounds of the large horn were heard, as well as the small horn, the flute, the pipes, the harp, and the drum.

The city resounded with cries of gladness. Then they brought forth the young man and he laid hold of the horns of the altar. And the kingship was given to him by the mouth of Zadok, the Priest. And he went out and they called his name David, for the name of a king came to him by the law. And they made him ride upon the mule of King Solomon and they led him around the city.

III And Zadok the Priest told David the King that he should serve no god but one, who is the Father of Israel. And he said: "If you will not hear the word of God, then the curses I now mention will fall upon you. Cursed you will be in the field, cursed you will be in the city. Cursed will be the fruit of your land, the fruit of your belly, the herds of your cattle, and the flocks of your sheep. The heavens above you shall become brass and the earth beneath you shall become iron. And God shall make a dark rain fall upon your land and dust shall descend from Heaven until it shall cover you up. And you will be smitten in battle before your enemies. And your dead body shall become food for the fowl and there shall be none to bury you. You shall grope about by day like a blind man in the darkness and you will find no one to help you in your trouble. You shall marry a wife and another man shall carry her away by force. You shall build a house but not dwell therein. And you shall plant a vineyard but not harvest the grapes thereof. All in all, you shall become a man of suffering and calamity. When the day dawns you shall say, 'would the evening had come' and when the evening comes you will say, 'would that morning had come.' And all these things shall come upon you if you will not hearken to the word of the Lord God of Israel, who rules everything."

IV Then Zadok explained the blessings that would come to he who acted upon the will of God: "You shall be blessed in the city and blessed in the field. Blessed shall be your house, blessed shall be all that is outside it, and blessed shall be the fruit of your belly. Blessed shall be the fruit of your land and the fountains of your waters. Blessed shall be your cattle runs and sheep flocks. Blessed shall be your granaries and barns. And you shall be blessed coming in and blessed going forth, and God shall bring to you the enemies who have risen up against you and they shall be broken beneath your feet, and God shall send his blessing to your house and to everything you have put your hand.

"And God shall multiply the children of your body, the fruit of your land, the births of your flocks and herds, and he shall open for you the storehouse of the heavens. And blessed rain shall fall upon you and shall bless the fruit of your labor. You shall lend unto many peoples, but you shall not borrow. You shall rule over many nations, but they shall not rule over you. Your honor shall rise up like the cedar and the morning star. And your brilliance shall be evident before every tribe of the people of Israel. Those who see you will have hearts that tremble before the bridle of your horses, the quiver of your bow, and the glitter of your shield. And they shall bow down to the face of the earth, for their hearts shall be terrified at the sight of your greatness."

And Zadok concluded, "Be a good man to the good and a reprover of sinners. Do justice to the poor and release them from the hand of him that does wrong. Deliver the forsaken and the man in misery and release him from the hand of him that causes him to suffer. Judge not with partiality, but judge righteously. When you judge, love not the gifts given by certain persons, and admonish the judges under you so that they are free from the taking of gifts, so they shall surely judge their neighbors in righteousness."

I And the firstborn children of the nobles of Israel, who were ordered to leave their country and go to Ethiopia, took counsel together. "Let us sorrow," they said, "over our Lady Zion." For in her they were bound to serve as unto God, and their sorrow was because they were having to leave her. "We have grown up under her blessedness," they said.

And as Azarayas, the son of Zadok the Priest, said, "Here is what we must do. We shall make a covenant to the end of our lives, and we will swear not to repeat it whether we live or whether we die, whether we are taken captive and whether we go forth."

Then he explained how they would take their Lady Zion with them on their journey. And all rose up and kissed him and said, "We will do what you have counseled us to do and whether we live or die we are with you for the sake of our Lady Zion." And one of them, the son of Benaiah, whose name was Zachariah, said, "You, Azarayas, can go into the House of God in place of your father Zadok, for the keys are often in your hand. You know the secret windows which King Solomon made and which no priest may enter except your father. Therefore, we shall have joy and our fathers shall have sorrow when our Lady Zion arrives with us in the country of Ethiopia."

And Azarayas said to his followers, "We shall have a carpenter fashion wood for a solid frame which will travel over land and sea, and resist sand, water, or bad weather. We will not speak of the matter to the King until we have traveled far."

So it was that they who were sent away made a plan which would compensate them for leaving their birthplace, their kinsfolk, and the people of their chosen city.

I And while Azarayas was asleep at night the Angel of the Lord appeared to him, and said, "Your Lord David shall speak to Solomon the King and shall ask him to offer up a sacrifice to the holy city Jerusalem and to Lady Zion, the holy and heavenly Tabernacle of the Law of God. And Solomon shall agree to this. And when the sacrifice is made, you shall bring forth the Tabernacle and carry it off. For, be it known that Israel has provoked God to wrath and for this reason He will have the Tabernacle removed."

And when Azarayas awoke from his dream he rejoiced and his heart and mind were clear. The Angel of the Lord had shown him in the night what he should do and had given him the strength to do it. After the sacrifice was made and everyone had returned to their houses and gone to sleep, Azarayas saw in a dream the Angel of the Lord once again. He stood above him like a pillar of fire and he filled the house with light. "Rise up," the Angel said, "and bring the wooden ark that you have made, for I will then open the doors of the Sanctuary and you may take the Tabernacle of God. And I will be your guide when you carry it away."

And Azarayas rose up straightaway and woke up his brethren, and they took the pieces of wood fashioned by a carpenter, and putting them in the place where they found Zion, the Tabernacle of God, they then took her away; and the Angel of the Lord was present and directed them to do so. They set the pieces of wood in the place where Zion had been and they covered them with the covering of Zion and then they shut the door which the Angel had opened and went back to their houses.

I Now when they bade farewell, Zion sat safely upon a wagon together with a pile of worthless things: dirty clothes and stores of every sort and kind. When all of the wagons were loaded and the horn was blown, the caravan masters gave their signal and the whole party began to depart. The city became excited; old men wailed and children cried out, widows wept and virgins lamented, for the mighty men of Israel had risen up and were leaving.

But the city did not weep for them alone, but because the soul of the city had been carried off with them. And although they did not know that Zion had been taken from them, they made no mistake in their hearts and they wept bitterly. There was not a house wherein there was not wailing; dogs howled and asses screamed and the people's tears were mingled. And it was as if the people had been slain with the edge of a sword.

And King Solomon was dismayed at the outcry of the city. He looked from the roof of the palace, and saw the whole city weeping. Solomon saw this with regret and he was deeply moved, and he trembled. "Ah," he lamented, "my glory is gone, my son goes as with the sinking sun, and the majesty of my city is no more."

For it was as Solomon's father once prophesied: "Ethiopia shall bow before Him and His enemies shall eat the dust."

And as he said: "Ethiopia shall stretch out her hands to God and He shall receive her with honor and the kings of the earth shall praise God."

II Solomon said to Zadok the Priest, "Go bring that covering which is upon Zion. For David's mother has said, 'Give us some of the fringe of the covering of Zion so that we may worship it.' And Zion, the Tabernacle of the Law of God, shall be a guide wherever you are. But it must always remain with us. And although it is not with you, you must honor it just the same." So David received from his father the offering, the covering of Zion, and a chain of gold. And they, the first-born of Solomon's kingdom, loaded the wagons, the horses, and the mules and they set out on their journey. And Michael, the Archangel, marched in front, and he spread out his wings and the caravans cut through the sea as upon dry land; and upon dry land he spread himself out like a cloud and shielded them from the fire of the sun. Moreover, no wagon was hauled, but the Angel raised them above the ground, and all who rode upon beasts were lifted up, and everyone traveled as a ship upon the sea when the wind blows. Thus did they travel, with none in front and none behind.

I They came in one day to the border of Egypt. And when the sons of Israel saw that they had come in one day a distance of thirteen days' march, they were amazed. For they were neither tired nor hungry. And no man nor beast had eaten or drunk their fill, so they knew that this thing was from God. Then they said to their King, "We have come to the water of Ethiopia. This is the Takkazi, which flows down from Ethiopia and waters the valley of Egypt." And there they set up their tents.

There they said to David their King that they knew of a great secret. And they told him what had been done and how it had been made to happen. And that God had made it good; and God was well pleased. "We directed our gaze and God directed it rightly. We meditated, and God directed our meditation."

Then Azarayas made a sign and told one of the others, "Dress our Lady so that our King may see her."

David drew breath three times and said, "Oh Lord, have you remembered us in your mercy? We, the castaways, the people whom thou has rejected? Have you now crowned us with your grace? And are we now the chosen ones?"

What can be said of the great joy in the camp of the King of Ethiopia? The people smote the ground with their feet and they clapped their hands together, and they stretched them out to heaven while casting themselves down to the ground and giving thanks to God in their hearts.

I And when David saw the Lady Zion, he proclaimed, "Wherever you go, salvation shall be in the house and in the field. Salvation shall be in the palace and the lowly hollow. Salvation shall be on the sea and on the desert sand. Salvation shall be in the high mountains and near hills. Salvation shall be in the heavens and on the earth. Salvation shall be on firm ground and in the empty abyss. Salvation shall be in death and in life, and it shall be in thy coming and thy going forth, and it shall cover our children and our tribe. Salvation shall be in the country and in the city, and shall touch both king and beggar, fruit and plant, man and beast, bird and creeping thing. And from this time forward, our Lady shall guide us, teach us, and give us understanding and wisdom, so that we may learn to praise each day, every day, every night, every hour, and all the length of time. "Rise up Zion, give us strength, our Queen, for you are the habitation of the God of Heaven." Thus spoke David the King, the son of Solomon, King of Israel. For the spirit of prophecy descended upon him. And he knew not what he said. And everyone who listened marvelled and said, "This son of a prophet has now become one himself."

II Then, early in the morning, the wagons rose up

and resumed their journey as before; and the people sang songs to Zion, and as the people of Egypt bade them farewell, they passed before them like shadows. And the people of Ethiopia took up their flutes, horns, and drums, and the noise of their instruments smashed the idols of Egypt. These were in the forms of men, dogs, and cats. And the idols fell off their pedestals and so broke into pieces. Figures of birds made of gold and silver fell down and were broken.

And the people came to the sea of Eritrea, the Red Sea, and when the holy Zion crossed over, the sea received them, and its waves were as whitecapped mountains which were split asunder, and the sea roared as the loudest of lions and made a noise like the winter thunder of Damascus. And the sea wor-shipped Zion. But while its billows grew into mountains, the wagons of Ethiopia were raised above the waves, and the sound of the breaking sea mingled with the sounds of the people's horns and drums. And whales and fishes came forth and worshiped Zion. And birds flapped through the froth, and there was joy in the sea of Eritrea.

And they arrived opposite Mount Sinai and remained there while the angels sang. The children of the earth raised their voices in song and psalm and their tambourines made joyful noise. Then they loaded their wagons and rose up and journeyed until they came to the country of Ethiopia. And as they travelled, Zion sent forth a light like that of the sun and it penetrated the darkness.

I When Zadok the Priest returned to Solomon the King, he found him sorrowful. And the King told him, "When the Queen of the South came here I had a night vision. It seemed as if I were standing in the chamber of Jerusalem. And the sun came down from heaven to the land of Judah and lighted it up with great splendor. And having tarried a time it went down and lighted up the country of Ethiopia, and it did not return to the land of Judah. And again the sun came down from heaven to the country of Judah and it lighted it up more brilliantly than before. But the Israelites paid no heed to it and they even wished to extinguish its light and now it rose below the earth in an unexpected place. And it illumined the country of Ethiopia."

Zadok the Priest then answered the King, saying, "Oh my Lord, Why did not you tell me this before? Something has happened to our Holy Lady, the heavenly Zion. Truly, I fear it."

And the King said, "Our wisdom is forgotten and our understanding is lost. The sun that appeared to me long ago when I slept with the Queen of Ethiopia was surely the symbol of the Holy Zion."

"The splendid covering that was lying upon Zion, I took it off," said Zadok. "But I did not trouble myself to look under the two coverings that remained."

"Go quickly and look at our Lady," said the King. "Examine her closely."

Zadok the Priest took the keys and opened the house of the sanctuary, but there he found nothing except the wooden boards which Azarayas had put there. These resembled the sides of the pedestal of Zion, but when Zadok saw them he fell forward on his face and dropped into a coma.

II When he did not return, Solomon sent someone to find him, and the messenger found the priest, whom he brought back to the King. When he awoke Zadok began to wail and the King knew from his cry that the Holy Zion was gone. Now he commanded a crier to go around, and soldiers seized their mounts and went forth to pursue the men who had taken Zion.

King Solomon swore, "As the Lord God of Israel lives, these men who have done this are men of death and not of life. For they deserve death now and that is what they shall receive."

Upon his command the King himself rose up and followed the road taken by the men of Ethiopia; and the mounted horsemen who went with him rode hard ahead and, at last, came to the country of Egypt. The soldiers of King Solomon questioned the people there and the Egyptians said to them, "Some days ago the travelers you seek came by here in wagons, which moved swifter than the eagles of the heavens."

The King's commander said to them, "How many days have passed since they left you?"

An Egyptian answered him,

"This is the ninth day since they left us."

When the commander returned to King Solomon, he told him, "Consider in your wisdom the distance these men have traversed. In one day they went thirteen days' distance; and now they are farther still. The people tell us that the company of men ride upon wagons suspended in the air. Surely this is not the power given to mortal men, but they must be guided by an angel."

"Was Zion with them?" King Solomon asked.

And the commander answered, "The people did not see anything like it."

Then Solomon turned his eyes to the heavens and he asked, "Why have you given your glory to another?"

I Now Solomon entered his tent and wept bitterly. Once again he turned his eyes upward. "Ah," he said, "I weep for myself. God has neglected us and has taken our Lady away. And now I know the reason. For our priests love the words of fables more than the words of scriptures. They love the sound of the harp more than the music of the psalter. They love the service more than the prayer. They love the world more than God. And they love food more than fasting to God. They love sleeping more than praising, they love dozing more than watching. They wish to gaze upon the face of their loved one more than upon the face of their God who loves them."

And now Solomon concluded, "Woe unto us. For we have loved the word of foolishness more than the word of the wise. We have loved the word of the fool more than the wisdom of the prophet. We were given glory and we have thrown it away. We were given riches and we have beggared ourselves. We have worn garments of finery, but we do not clothe the soul with prayer."

And while Solomon was saying these things he continued to weep and the tears ran down his cheeks. In this moment of penance he heard a voice: "Solomon, why are you thus sorrowful? What has happened is the will of God. Zion has not been given to one who is foreign but to your own firstborn son. Comfort yourself with this and return to your house. And do not be so sad. For the will of God is done and not the will of man."

And then Solomon saw the Angel of God appear before him, and the Angel said to him: "As for yourself you shall build the house of God and if you keep his commandment and do not serve other gods you shall be beloved by God."

II When Solomon came back to the city of Jerusalem he wept there with the elders but they spoke to the King and said, "Do not be sorrowful concerning this thing, for we know that nothing happens without the will of God. For in the time of Eli the Priest, even before our fathers had asked for a king, the Philistines carried Zion into their camp. And they set the Tabernacle in their city and placed it before their god Dagon.

"And Dagon was broken into pieces and destroyed and turned to dust. Then the fruit of their land was devoured by mice and the people became miserable with pestilence and sores. The people gathered together with their priests, magicians, and stargazers, who told them that their punishment had come upon them because of the stolen Zion. So then the people knew that they must take her back to her city, her country, and her house. And sacrifices were made and sixty mice cast in gold and also sixty figures of the tribe of man. And these offerings were given to Zion.

"But the Philistine priests now wished to determine in which direction to send the Tabernacle. So they placed together two she-camels, yoked side by side. If they were to march straight for Jerusalem the Philistines would know that God had relented and would cause them no more suffering.

But if the camels turned back to the place from whence they started, then the Philistines would know that God was still angry with them and that their punishment would continue.

"And those camels made their way straight to the country of Judah. They came to the threshing floor of the house of your kinsmen. And those gathered there were the men of the house of Dan, and they did not do homage to Zion for they regarded her as their destroyed god. They cut up the wood of the wagon and made the camels into sacrifices, but they returned Zion to her place.

"And while Zion was in her house Samuel the Prophet had visions and gave prophecies which were directed by God, who was pleased with Samuel's action; and he ruled Israel for forty-eight years. And Samuel anointed Saul as King, and he reigned forty years. But when the Philistines fought with Saul and conquered him, and he died with Nathan, his son, there were still left other sons who wished to carry Zion away with them now that their father and their brother were dead. They wished to hide her in the valley of Gilboa, so that your father David might not take her. Again, when your father reigned rightly over Israel he took her from the city of Samaria and brought her here to Jerusalem. So, concerning the coming and going of Zion to the country of Ethiopia, or any other country, if God has willed it, there is no one who could prevent her from leaving or returning. It is all in God's good pleasure. Do not let your heart be sad but comfort yourself in the wisdom which God has given you and therefore Israel. For wisdom is a strange thing. And just as a lamp is not the sun, so the word of a fool is not the word of a wise man. And just as smoke is to the eye an unripe fruit to the tooth and vinegar unto honey, so the words of fools are not beneficial to the wise."

Old Rastas—who remember the political persecutions of their people in the times of tribal war that swept across the island and are willing to share their stories, permitting an outsider to hear them—are hard to come by. Such histories have not been widely shared. But they should be, because they represent something Biblical: the persecution of the Israelites as equated with the suffering of the African people. An elder Rasta, Spreeboy, tells what it was like to see Haile Selassie in a vision and in the flesh, and what this meant to the Rasta community in Jamaica. It is an emotional, moral, and spiritual encounter that is all the more impressive because it is true. When Spreeboy speaks it is as if the pages of the Kebra Nagast had turned back into spoken words.

Spreeboy, whose given name is not known to anyone in Castle Gordon, is a Rastafarian elder whose flesh is drawn against his facial bones like a knot so that his eyes are startling and seem to burn within their sockets. Spreeboy is seventy-something, no one knows for sure; but he can hop up a sixty-foot coconut palm and pluck coconuts the way he did when he was fourteen.

His dreads are gray now, but his eyes, like those of a cat,

are clear—he says it is because "I smoke weed." Most Rastas believe that herb prevents glaucoma. Spreeboy tends a small farm in the town of Mason Hall, located in the hills above Castle Gordon. Once or twice a week, he shows up with a black "scandal bag" full of jackfruit, alligator pear, pine (pineapple), ripe banana, soursop, sweetsop, and guava.

For these gifts of love, Spreeboy refuses money, but, in keeping with some old rite, he accepts tobacco, batteries, and lighter fluid.

One day Spreeboy announces that he wants to tell me history; that is, his story. He begins not with the incidental fact of birth, but with a vision of Haile Selassie I.

Sitting in an Edwardian-style bamboo chair in the thatch-roofed bar at Blue Harbour, Spreeboy's pale eyes gleam greenish gold, his skin the color of light coffee, his face an image of wild concentration, ever on the verge of either laughter or moral outrage. He looks, without trying, like a desert prophet, a mad-eyed son of the Ethiopian sand. His eyes, deeply hypnotic, are set in a perpetual stare. He is perhaps the oldest Rasta in the parish. What he could tell, if he wanted to tell it . . . but now he begins:

"This happened long ago, well before the visit of the Emperor to Jamaica, which was in April of 1966."

Momentarily, his cat's eyes shine in remembrance. His expression turns inward, as if he is not really here but somewhere else. When he begins again, his voice rapturous, his eyes aglow, he is very far off, it seems to me, in another world, the world of mythology.

"It was a land of brilliant sun that I recognized, though I knew I had never been there in the flesh."

His voice purrs with a velvety softness. He goes on, eyes tranced, voice dropping to a whisper.

"As I say, the sun was brilliant but it carried no heat. My face turned to the northeast; there the Emperor was, and he took three steps to the left and held up his fist in which he clenched a length of rope. 'Marvel not,' he said. Then, 'Go and read Revelation 5 and 6.' And that was all that he said at that time.

"When I became awake, I hurried to the King's Street Bible Museum in Kingston. There was a Bible there that I could read, and this is what it said:

> And I saw in the right hand of him that sat on the throne a book written within and on the backside, sealed with seven seals.
> And I saw a strong angel proclaiming with a loud voice, Who is worthy to open the book, and to loose the seals thereof?
> And no man in heaven, nor in earth, neither under the earth, was able to open the book, neither to look thereon.
> And I wept much, because no man was found worthy to open and to read the book, neither to look thereon.
> And one of the elders saith unto me, Weep not: behold, the Lion of the tribe of Judah, the Root of David, hath prevailed to open the book, and to loose the seven seals thereof.

Spreeboy breathes deeply before reciting the sixth chapter of Revelation:

> And I saw when the Lamb opened one of the seals, and I heard, as it were the noise of thunder, one of the four beasts saying, Come and see.
> And I saw, and behold a white horse: and he that sat on him had a bow; and a crown was given unto him: and he went forth conquering and to conquer.
> And when he had opened the second seal, I heard the second beast say, Come and see.

Now pausing and looking at me, Spreeboy wants to know if I am following what he is saying.

"You know Revelation?"

He goes on, "It is the Emperor himself who is loosing the seals, and telling us what is to come. In my vision he is clothed in a golden knit shirt, milk white short pants, and there are two wound scars on the inside of his palms."

"The same scars," I add, "that Rita Marley saw when she first laid eyes on him."

Spreeboy claps his hands together.

"That was the twenty-first of April, nineteen-hundred-and-sixty-six."

The date is etched in his mind, and I realize that he is there now; not here with me, though he is talking with me and making conversation. His voice drops into that mesmerizing tone.

"I saw His Majesty's plane appear out of the northeast. And, as the plane came in, it was wreathed in a thick cloud of darkness. Then the darkness was washed away with a flood of water. When the airplane started to descend, there was light."

Spreeboy waits, allowing his words to sink in. For a while he is quiet, neither speaking nor moving. Just staring.

A few minutes pass. I ask Spreeboy if he knows the story of Haile Selassie's meeting with King George; how he cut the apple into thirteen parts.

Spreeboy looks up, surprised.

"Who tell you that?" he demands.

"Michael Higgins."

He seems to think about this for a little while.

"There is more to that, you know. More than Michael tell you."

Then he elaborates, telling me that, "King George tossed that apple, and with his sword, divided it into twelve sections in the air. When it was the Emperor's turn, His Majesty tossed the apple, cut it up, midair as before, but one section of apple, the thirteenth piece, was stuck to the point of his sword."

The twelve tribes, plus one.

"But now," he continues, "I must tell you how the Emperor was received by the big shots of Jamaica. As you must know, he was the first king to ever set foot in an eighteenth-century building on the island of Jamaica. His words bear witness to what happened there at that time, for he said clearly, and for all to hear: 'How can a man resist such an invitation of love and compassion?' He then asked for the Minister of Justice and nobody called forth this minister, so Justice was not there."

Spreeboy stops talking. After the appropriate silence, I ask him if the Emperor was speaking in English. He responds quickly. "He spoke in Amharic, a language we could not understand because those words had long ago been beaten out of us. His words yet ring in my ears," he whispers, and then adds, "The Emperor said only one more thing, and I will remember it until the day that I die. He said, 'Holy priests, be still and realize that I am He.'"

For a long while, he is quiet. A car horn on the road seems oddly out of place, as does the static pulse of a nearby radio.

After a long, meditative silence, he stands up.

"I will come back another time, and tell you of Marcus Mosiah Garvey," Spreeboy announces, and then he says goodbye in a small, soft voice, and leaves by the gate, back straight, eyes ahead, his age concealed to all.

The Kebra Nagast states that what we call fate or chance is really the interaction of God with events on the human scene. How we choose to meet these events, however, is on the personal plane of destiny, each man's or woman's free choice to meet, fulfill, sacrifice, nullify, or evade. In other words, like Solomon, when he discovers the loss of Lady Zion, we have the free will to make decisions that will affect us for the rest of our lives.

There is a man we fear, a man who roams about the streets of Port Maria. Americans would call him deranged, insane, at loose ends, out of his skull. However, on the island of Jamaica, such people are simply known as madmen. The name is for either gender, and there is no irony or sardonicism in it—it is an unequivocal statement of fact.

In America and other "first world" nations, there are institutions for madmen, but there are few of these in Jamaica. So the mad roam about freely, their arms flailing, their cries thrown to eternity, their unsightly, soiled clothing hanging in rags and fringes as they parade upon the streets, dancing the dance of the famished, the foolish, the furious and, occasionally, the criminally dangerous.

Normally, however, madmen are seen for what they are:

people so worn down in every way that a meal of garbage out of a can is better to them than a bowl of hot rice. You see them hollering to heaven about the condition of their life. You hear them raising a litany that would make brother Job's seem like a child's Christmas list.

In our village of Port Maria, the resident madman who roars up and down the streets, castigating the air, is a diminutive man by the name of Runaway.

For more than ten years now he has been my nemesis, with his cutlass carving the air over his head. As he comes down Cock Street or Warner Lane, we see him flailing at the sky and throwing out a mountain of invective about white people in general, and me in particular.

Those who see him ignore him as he passes by, roaring and raging. I would hate to be near that cutlass windmill, that Vesuvius of words.

No one else seems to care about the man's grotesque anger, his verbal torrent—no one, in fact, seems to even hear it but me.

There really isn't anything I can do about Runaway except remove myself.

One day I am reasoning with my old friend Raggy.

"Listen, Ger," he says affectionately, "to me you are a Jamaican, but for two things."

I chuckle. "And what are they?"

"Well, number one, I don't think you've seen a dead."

I nod that this is true. I have not seen a person dying or dead while I have been in Jamaica. A great many things have been glimpsed and seen, but not that. I have witnessed a riot in Kingston, where dogs were released to terrorize the crowds at a concert gone out of control. I have seen an African-style settlement of a land claim, where the two families met on the line and threw rocks at each other. I have seen what could not be explained otherwise as anything but a ghost. I have seen mayhem and madness, beauty and poetry. But I have not seen a dead person and I have not spoken to a madman.

"And what is number two?"

"Number two is you haven't spoken to Runaway."

"Does it have to be Runaway? I'd sooner speak with a dead."

Raggy's eyes narrow to a tiny squint as he bursts out laughing.

"A true. A true," he sputters, trying to control himself.

"When was the last time you saw a dead?" I ask him.

"All the while," he answers. Then he tells me that he used to work in a morgue where he had to "tenderize" the bodies for burial.

"Tenderize?"

"Beat them into shape."

He laughs a little, then grows serious.

He remarks, "You would say I massaged them. But what I really did was beat them with a stick to soft them up."

"So does this have to do with my becoming an honorary Jamaican?" I chide.

He answers back, slipping into patois, "Even likkle baby like fe see a dead. It good for the heart, mon."

"Seeing the dead, or perhaps knowing you're still alive?"

"Seeing a dead," Raggy insists, "do something fe a mon."

"Should I go to the morgue this afternoon?" I tease.

He wobbles with laughter.

"Wha' haffa 'oppen a-go 'oppen," he concludes.

Raggy pats me on the back. "It just so."

The British used to call the island Doctor Jamaica. The name is appropriate.

In my life, so far, I have had the good luck to meet whatever my heart required. So, as it happens, both things that Raggy's suggested—seeing a dead person and meeting a madman—occurred within the next twenty-four hours, just before my departure from the island to return to the States.

Riding in Ernie's bus, the Irie One, in Montego Bay, we find ourselves in a downpour. The bus ahead of us, trying to avoid an oncoming vehicle and sliding on the pavement, overturns.

Ernie stops and the police come to officiate the accident. For some reason, I am the first person to set eyes on a man who has fallen out of the overturned bus. The man looks at me, his eyes glancing deeply into my own. Then he closes them, and, just like that, dies. Soon after some people on the roadside cover his face gently with a banana leaf. This is an old custom signifying, as it is said, "a dead."

On the way back to Port Maria, I am wondering why the man looked so directly into my eyes. He seemed to see no one else.

Why me?

The feeling of his eyes resting deeply on mine, the eyes of

a stranger at once no longer strange, is not something I can easily forget.

Nor do I want to.

My son-in-law, Sava, says it this way: "Some people alive are dead; some people dead are alive."

The same day, as fate will have it, I meet Runaway, face to face. It happens like this. As soon as Ernie arrives in Port Maria, I step out into the sun, and there, almost in front of me, as if stationed there to meet me, is Runaway. He has his trusty cutlass, and he is swiping the air with it, raging about white people.

He comes on closer. I have my back to the wall, literally. He gets within a few feet of me, roaring.

The machete whispers at my ear.

Whoosh-swheer-shweep.

I feel the death breath of the machete. The smell of Runaway, the rankness of him, is something else. And there is less than an arm's length between us.

As with the dead, I find myself drawn into Runaway's eyes.

I look into him as if he were a soulmate.

I cease to notice anything about him, his smell, his clothes, his face. I only see the penetrating eyes locking on me, fixing me to him. Out of the corner of my eye, I see the arm with the cutlass rise. The blade glimmers in the sun.

Then, something compels me to step, not backward but forward. Closing the distance between us, I take more two strategic steps.

The cutlass slowly drops to his side like the gate of a bridge; the point glances against my elbow, but it does not cut my skin.

Runaway's eyes glare ferociously. A huge crowd seems to have grown out of nowhere. I feel the pressure of the curious. But, still, there is really only one thing that I am aware of, and that is the eyes of Runaway. Nothing else seems to exist, just the twin points of the madman's gaze. I am hooked to him as he is hooked to me.

And so we stare.

At last, my lips move of their own volition, and I say to him, "Runaway, I am told that you are a kind and gentle soul. Why, I ask myself, over all of these years that we have seen one another, have I not gone forward to meet you? Why have I not come out so that we might speak to one another, man to man? I haven't an answer any more than you have an answer now for the thing you are doing—pushing a knife into the belly of your brother."

Runaway's mouth pinches, flickers. His stare softens. He stifles something like the sob of a child, then catches himself. His voice is smooth as butter, soft as oil.

"You are a gentleman," he says in his cut-glass English. "A gentleman is one deserving of honor, requiring a greeting far greater than my humble office allows. I beg you, gracious sir, to consider my unpardonable error and let these many years to slide past in forgetfulness. I beg your forgiveness."

Then bowing backwards as he moves away, Runaway

takes his leave. I watch him as he returns from whence he came.

Something sacred has occurred. Some small miracle of confidence.

Raggy, when he hears of the incident that night, reminds me that "Even a dead have something to say, but a madman is no more mad than hungry. Give him a bowl of rice, and his tongue will work on food rather than insult. Enough people in this land just want to live. We go along every day, taking this life for granted. Give thanks and praises for life, mon. Don't bow your head. Don't look down at your portion. Look up into the eyes of the man next to you, for that individual could be God himself. Yes, it is just so."

Leaving the next morning, going back to the States, I promise myself never to betray the confidence given to me by this island. We walk so thin a line, I think, between the dead and the mad, that our lives are made of nothing so dense as flesh nor so light as spirit. We are made of each, but the choice is ours whether, as Bob Marley said, we wish to be as light as a feather or as heavy as lead, whether we wish to live in heaven or hell, whether we wish to sing with the angels or dance with the devils. The choice is ours.

I And Solomon lived for eleven years after Zion was taken away from him; and then his heart turned aside from the love of God. He forgot his wisdom and spent his time among many women. He loved the daughter of Pharaoh the King of Egypt, whose name was Makshara. Solomon brought her into the house which he had made and there in the ceiling were images of the sun, moon, and stars. The beams were made of brass and the roof of silver. The stone walls were red with black and brown with white and green. The floor was made of blocks of sapphire and sardius. There Solomon and his wife Makshara spent their time.

Now the Queen had idols which her father had given her and she knelt before them, and when Solomon saw her he did not rebuke her. This made God angry with him and thus Solomon forgot his wisdom. And the children of Israel joined themselves to Solomon's wife in the service of idols. Solomon found pleasure in hearing the foolish service, and the Queen spoke to him with honeyed words and with the turning of the face; and with actions of this kind she enticed him to the evil of her work. And as the deep sea draws down into its depths the man who cannot swim, even so did that woman wish to submerge Solomon the King. She told him, "It is good to worship the gods like my father and all the kings of Egypt who were before my father."

So Solomon answered her, "They call gods the things which have been made by the hands of carpenter, potter, painter, and sculptor? These are not gods but the work of the hand of man. We worship the holy God of Israel and our Lady, the holy and heavenly Zion, the Tabernacle of the Law of God."

"Your son has carried away your Lady Zion," she answered. "This son, who springs from an alien people which God has not commanded you to marry. Your son's mother is an Ethiopian woman, who is not akin to your country."

"Very well," Solomon answered, "and aren't you of that race? And your kin, her kin? And aren't all of you the children of Ham? As for Zion, the will of God has been performed. They have her so that they may worship her. As for me, I will not worship your idols."

II Now the wife of Solomon treated him disdainfully, and she beautified and scented herself for him, but kept at one remove. He asked her, "What shall I do? Ask me and I will give you what you wish. You must be gracious to me once again."

She did not answer him. And he repeated to her the words that he had said. Finally she spoke, "Promise me by the God of Israel that you will do what I ask you to do." And Solomon swore to her that he would give her whatever she asked and would do whatever she wanted him to do. Then she tied a scarlet thread in the middle of the door of the house of her gods. And she brought three locusts and set them in the house also.

She said to Solomon, "Come to me without breaking the scarlet thread and kill these locusts by pulling off their heads." When he had done so she said to him, "I will now do your will, for you have done mine. You have sacrificed to my gods and you have now worshiped them."

III Who was wiser than Solomon? And yet he was seduced by the gentle voice of a sweet woman. For even though God commanded the children of Israel not to marry strange women so they wouldn't be corrupted by them through their gods, Solomon did not pay heed. Nor did David, who was stronger than Samson but was also seduced by a woman. Who was handsomer than Amnon, who was seduced by Tamar, the daughter of David, his father? And Adam was the first creation of God and yet he was seduced by Eve, his wife. And thus are we all the children of Eve.

And so Solomon sinned a great sin through the worship of idols, and though he was once a wise man, he became a fool. And his sin is written down in the book of the prophets.

I Solomon's days were sixty years when a sickness attacked him. And his days were not as the days of David his father, but they were twenty years fewer. And the Angel of Death came and smote him in the foot. And the angel said to him, "Harken to what I say, for God has sent me. From being a wise man you have turned into a fool, and from being wealthy you have become poor, and from being a king you've turned into a common person, and all because you have broken the commandment of God. You held this lightly, thinking you were wiser than God and believing you would have many male children. But the foolishness of God is wiser than the wisdom of men. And you shall know that from your seed shall come forth a Savior who shall deliver you and all those who come after you. Just as Joseph brought his kinfolk from the famine, which was the first Sheol in that land, so shall the Savior bring you out of Sheol. And as Moses brought his kinsmen out of Egypt, so shall you be brought out of Sheol. And as Joshua brought his people into the land of promise, so shall the Savior bring you into the garden of delight. And as you have built the house of God, so shall churches be built in His honor.

"Know that your Salvation was created in the belly of Adam. And it began in the form of a pearl before Eve. The pearl did not go into Cain or Abel but it went forth from the belly of Adam into the belly of Seth. And then it went into those who were the firstborn, and came to Abram. And it did not go from Abram into his firstborn, Ishmael, but it tarried and went into Isaac the pure. And it did not go into his firstborn, the arrogant Esau, but it went into Jacob the humble. And it did not enter into his firstborn, the erring Reuben, but into Judah, the innocent. And it did not go forth from Judah until four sinners had been born, but it came to Fares the patient. And from him the pearl went to the firstborn until it came into the belly of Jesse, your grandfather. And then it waited until six men of wrath had been born, and it then went to the seventh, David, your innocent and humble father.

"Now the pearl of your salvation will pass through many generations until it will reach him who shall be the salvation of all mankind. He who is crucified without sin and who rises without corruption. He who goes into Sheol and tears down its walls. So therefore, none of you who have carried the pearl shall be destroyed. From Adam to the Savior, and from that time forward, all shall be saved. And whether it be men or women, all who have carried the pearl shall be saved, for by it they shall be made holy and pure. And Zion, taken up by your firstborn, shall be the salvation of the people of Ethiopia forever; and the pearl shall be carried in the belly of Rehoboam your son, and shall be the savior of all the world.

"I am Gabriel the Angel, the protector of those who shall carry the pearl from the body of Adam, even to the belly of Hannah. And the Angel Michael has been commanded to keep Zion, wheresoever she goes; and the Angel Uriel shall keep the wood of the thicket, which shall be the cross of the Savior. The Angel Michael is with Zion, and with David who has taken the throne of David your father. And I am with the pure pearl which shall reign forever, and which is in your second son Rehoboam; and the Angel Uriel is with your youngest son, Adrami."

Solomon stretched out both his hands and said to the Angel, "My Lord, is the coming of the Savior near or far off?"

"He will come, three and thirty generations from your kin. But Israel will hate their Savior because he will work miracles before them. And they will crucify him and kill him and he shall rise up again and deliver them. And behold, I tell you plainly, he will not leave his kinsmen, those by whom the pearl has been carried, in Sheol."

"I would ask you one more question," said Solomon. "Will the people of Israel be blotted out after the coming of the Savior?"

And the Angel of God answered him, "When they have poured out His blood on the wood of the cross they shall then be scattered all over the world."

And Solomon said, "I weep for my people. And of myself, I have this to say: Of what use is a king if he has done no good upon the earth for the poor? His path to the grave is the same as theirs; and their path in the deep is the same. Of what use is a man? The breath which we breathe is for so short a time. And the beat of our heart and the spark of our mind shall pass away, and thus we become dust. And that understanding which is in our mind vanishes when our soul is poured out; and so does our body become worms and degradation. So that when the heat of our body grows cold we pass away like a cloud. Therefore is the strength of kings blotted out and so do we pass away like shadows, and, having passed away in death, our name is then forgotten. And no trace of us can be found. After three generations of our children there is no one to remember our name. And who shall then recall our good deeds, our errors, our loves, and grant us our mortality?"

II And then Solomon the King turned to face Rehoboam his son. And he told him not to bow down to strange gods, and to withhold himself from evil, and do only the things that are good so that his days on earth would be many. And then he said to him, "Write me in the roll of the Book, and lay it in the chest." And he said to Zadok the Priest, "Anoint my son and make him King, as my father David made me King while he was alive." Then they set Rehoboam upon the King's mule and the city resounded with cries, but before Rehoboam could return to his father Solomon died. And they laid Solomon in the tomb of his father David and there was great mourning for him, for in those days and those to come his wisdom would always be remembered.

And when seven days had passed Rehoboam called for the mourning to cease. And the people of Israel gathered before Rehoboam and complained to him that they wished their labor to be lessened. "Your father," they said, "made heavy the hewing of wood, the dressing of stone, and the bringing down of cedarwood."

So Rehoboam took counsel and he was told by his old counselors, "Answer the people graciously." At present he was young, they told him, and he could not do with the people what he wished. Now his young counselors wished him not to show a timid face, but to address the people with bold words and to make everyone obey him.

Thus did Rehoboam speak to the elders of Israel, "Nothing shall diminish your labor, and if you will not do my command I will take your cattle and capture your children. I will seize your cities and your fields; I will take your wells, and your gardens, and the fruit of your crops. I will bind your loved ones in chains of iron and feed your riches to my servants. Your women shall adorn the house of my nobles. For the whole of this land was given to David my grandfather, and to my father after him; and God has given it to me after my fathers and I will make you serve me as you served them. Now take counsel and obey me."

Then the elders of Israel withdrew, and there was rebellion in them. "Have we no one else whom we can make King?" they asked. And they took up the weapons of war and fled to the city of Samaria. There they cast lots among themselves and a king was chosen from the House of Ephraim; and so Jeroboam was made king. And thus was the kingdom separated from Rehoboam, the son of Solomon.

They called Rehoboam King of Judah, and they called the King of Samaria King of Israel.

And of the generations of Rehoboam to Joachim, there were forty-one. And Jacob took to wife Yohada, the wife of Eli, and he begat by her Joseph the carpenter, who was the betrothed of Mary. And there was born of her the Word, the Light of Light, the God of God, the Son of the Father who has delivered all of us who have believed in him, for he is a lover of man, and unto him praise will extend forever.

I Now it came to pass that when David the son of Solomon returned with the Ark of the Covenant, he met his mother Makeda and she granted that he should be King of Ethiopia. She saw that he was his father's son, and she spoke then of the great wisdom she had learned from the King.

"Wisdom," she said. "I have drunk from her but have not fallen. Because of her I have dived down into the great sea and have seized in her depths a pearl whereby I am rich. I went down like an iron anchor and I found a lamp which burned in the dark water. And I came up to breathe the air of understanding. I went to sleep in the depths of the sea and lay be- calmed as upon my own bed wherein I dreamed a dream. And it seemed to me that there was a star in my womb, and I marvelled at it, and I laid hold upon it and made it strong in the splendor of the sun. I went into the deep well of knowledge and drew for myself the water of wisdom. I went into the blaze of the sun, and I made a shield for myself cast from my understanding. And my confidence is not for myself only but for all of those who travel in the footprints of wisdom, for the Kingdom of Ethiopia and all the nations around us."

And the Queen said to her son, "Speak to me of what you know."

I And Azarayas, the son of Zadok the Priest, spoke for King David when he said, "We see that the country of Ethiopia is better than the country of Judah.

"Your waters are good and are given without payment, the air is fine without fans, and the wild honey is as plentiful as the dust of the marketplace.

"You are black of face and God is the light in your heart, therefore nothing can do you harm. You do not touch meat that dies of itself, nor blood, nor the bodies torn by wild animals.

"But now you must hearken to God, the holy one of Israel, and do his good pleasure, for he has rejected our nation and has chosen you. Hearken well unto His command which I will now declare to you.

"Let no one overcome another by violence. Take no possession of your neighbor. You shall not revile each other, nor oppress each other, and you shall not quarrel amongst yourselves. And if, by chance, an animal belonging to your neighbor should come to you, then make it go back to him. And if a man is carrying a heavy load, you should not pass on your way until you have helped him to lift it up or lighten it for him, for he is your brother.

"You shall not turn aside the rights of those who are unfortunate. You shall not take bribes to turn aside the right and bear false witness. You must remember to treat all creatures both wild and domestic with kindness, so that your days may be long upon the earth. And when you shall harvest, you shall not take all, but will leave something for the stranger in your city. And you shall not work impurity, nor judge with partiality, nor deal with one another oppressively. For the law of God has commanded that there will be a curse on the worker of evil. And over and above all of these things you shall worship no other gods. Blessed are those who listen to the voice of God and obey his commandments, and blessed are those who turn aside from those who do evil. Blessed is the one who gives up his possessions unselfishly and who teaches others to do so as well.

"And this is what you shall eat: Every creature with a cleft hoof and the creatures that chew the cud. And those which you shall not eat among those so mentioned are the camel and the hare.

"The pig you shall not eat, for the hoof is cleft, but they do not chew the cud.

"Whatever is in the water with fins and scales, you shall eat.

"Whatever is unclean, that which lives in the shell, you shall not eat.

"Among birds, you may eat everything that is clean; but those that are unclean, those that eat meat themselves, you shall not eat.

"You shall not eat things that fly and spring and have six feet, namely grasshoppers and locusts.

"Now these things we have declared to you, so that you may be blessed in your country, which God has given you because of the heavenly Zion. Because of Her you have been chosen and blessed. He will bless the fruit of your land and He will multiply your cattle and He will protect them in everything wherein they are to be protected.

"And as for you, My Lady, Makeda, your wisdom is good, and it surpasses the wisdom of men. There is none that can be compared with you, not only in the intuition of women, but the understanding of your heart is deeper than that of men. And there is no one who compares to you in the abundance of understanding except my Lord, Solomon.

"For you have drawn the Tabernacle of the Law of God, overthrown the house of idols, cleansed what was unclean among your people, and driven away from them that which God would not bless."

So ended the speech of Azarayas to Queen Makeda.

I And Azarayas said, "Bring here the trumpets and let us go to Zion, for there we will make a new kingdom for our lord David."

Then he took the oil of sovereignty and anointed David. And they blew horns, pipes, and trumpets, and beat drums, and there was singing and dancing, and the people were glad of heart. And all the men and women of Ethiopia were present, the small and the great, and those to whom glory was given in that sunlit land.

So in this way the kingdom of David, the son of Solomon, was renewed in Mount Makeda, in the House of Zion, where the Law was established for the first time by the King of Ethiopia, and where it flourished because of the devoutness of the people.

II And the people of Ethiopia prospered because of their belief in the Lord; and when the Pearl, the Son of the Lord, was born, He wrought many signs and wonders.

He raised the dead and healed the sick, and He made the eyes of the blind see again.

And He performed miracles which were written down, and miracles which were not recorded, and therefore miracles which no one knows.

But the wicked of Israel thought He was a man and they were envious of Him, and they decided to kill him. Yet as we know, He was only a man so that the people might see Him. For when the Pearl passed into His mother, He was not visible, but He became so only because mortal man had need of Him, and had to see Him as other men are seen.

And the people of Ethiopia were loved by God because the Savior of the World, His Son, was beloved by them. And in the time when He was reborn to redeem Adam, they believed the signs and wonders that He wrought, though the people of Israel did not believe them. And for this reason God has deeply loved the people of Ethiopia.

The Nyabinghi runs like a heartbeat through the ceremonial affairs of the Rasta community. This African/Jamaican celebration incorporates singing, chanting, poem saying, drumming, and speech giving, and is based upon the Solomonic virtue of sharing what one has with everyone.

Beneath the bridge over the White River in Ocho Rios, city of the eight rivers, a big Nyabinghi is about to happen. This is sometimes called a "groundation celebration," or ceremony, in which the African heartbeat foundation chant and drum music form the closest tie that Rastas might admit to a church service. Their sacred ceremony—a "churchical expression," as someone said—may last for a few days or even longer, usually as a moment of praise in the calendar of Rastafari. The date for such an event could honor Emperor Haile Selassie's birthday, July 23; his coronation, November 1930; or his visit to Jamaica in April 1966. On the other hand, a Nyabinghi may occur at any time of year as a way of praising "the most I."

Although the celebration is one of light, there is in Nyabinghi a shared dark night of the soul, perhaps a lingering memory of slavery, of suffering when drumming was outlawed by the colonial powers. Here in the unmistakable "rid-dim" of the burru skin drums, the old world of Babylon crumbles, beaten down by chant, rhythmic pounding, and exultation of the heart. Yet even in the affirmation of salvation, the darkness remains.

Where does the darkness of humankind come from? The Devil? A malformed or, so to say, bad seed? The Kebra Nagast suggests both of these possibilities, the interpretation being that the experience of evil is both a choice and a chance. It is a matter of "joy or blues," as Ziggy Marley so aptly put it.

Bob Marley's message on this subject, which is at the heart of Nyabinghi, appears in many of his songs and much of what he said in his interviews. "Out of the darkness must come out the light," he said. "And if your night should turn to day/a lot of people would run away," and "Devils are real people, and capitalism and penalism [are a] type of devilism and draculizing." All of these unfathomables come to mind at a Nyabinghi. The air is spirited with angels, the earth dancing with devils, the mind overrun with fantasies of heaven and hell:

> Think you're in heaven, but you're living in hell
> Time alone, oh, time will tell

The night is loud with hand drumming, fire leaping, people talking, water rushing, traffic gushing, and the more usual sounds of the night—children crying, radios blaring, the sea crashing. For the White River empties into the sea, and we are at the turning of the tide, where it crashes up, exchanging salt for sweet.

Speakers appear on the makeshift stage under the arch of the bridge.

An old dreadlock Rasta stands suddenly before the crowd, using his cane to thump out the ricochet ramming of the Nyabinghi drums. For a moment, nothing is heard except the crackle of fire, the pop of exploding wood. Climbing smoke makes a blue mist that twines with the fog rising off the river. It is an unearthly scene.

The old man dread speaks a poem, thundering his carved Nyabinghi cane at the end of each line:

> From a place of mist and much rain
> Comes the pirate, Henry Morgan.
> There is cold gray sky in those eyes.
> Ah, yes, Judgment Time is come.
>
> Before the cane there was the rain;
> Before the rain there was a bird.
> Before the bird there was the Ark.
> Ah, yes, Judgment Time.
>
> Come, little children, put down your pirate books.
> Come to me and learn the truth.
> An eye-for-an-eye, a tooth-for-a-tooth
> Makes for one-eyed, one-toothed pirates.
> Ah, yes, Judgment Time.

He finishes, shaking his locks, matted as old gray moss. His eyes are fire-rimmed and the flames of the Nyabinghi lick at the heels of his bare feet. He moves off and a youth takes his place, an eleven-year-old Rasta, whose sweet face shines in the light of the log-devouring fire.

A fire dancer appears. Tongues of flame lick at him. Then he dives and rolls and puts out the fire, dropping flames like small blue snakes at his feet. He puts flames on his arms, immersing his head and neck. Then he dashes off, burning like a Roman candle, only to come back, supple and smooth, wet with river water. Now he pours white rum into his mouth and lights his tongue like a wick, weaving around the crowd, snorting fire like a dragon.

The youthful Rasta on stage waits for the end of this fire-foolery, when the dancer, amid small sputters of applause, has tamed fire; has joined himself in the judgment; and has anointed himself, as in Isaiah, Jeremiah, and Daniel.

Now, it is the youth's turn. Shaking his young locks, he sings out:

> I go and play my ten string among Nyabinghi.
> I go among men who don't live up, but who live down.
> I move among false brethren, wolves in sheep clothing;
> men who wear lock and beard, but who bear the likeness
> of strangers. I know Jah children come in all shape and size,
> and whether high man or low man, makes no difference.
> But I have seen the blood of generations on the lips
> of the false righteous. False prophets are among us now.
> The truth of that is to know it, to speak of it,

to sing of it; for he who feels it knows it

and he who does not feel it does not know it.

So the prophet Bob Marley saith, "Your best friend could be your

worst enemy

and your worst enemy your best friend."

Listen, my brothers, and look around you.

Is there someone out there drinking blood like a vampire?

Can you hear it, the sucking, the lapping of blood?

When he is finished, there is silence under the bridge. The drums have stopped; the talking has dwindled. The night presides. The youth stands humbled. The people keep looking at him, as if trying to understand how one so young can overstand so much.

The next person to speak on the makeshift stage is a middle-aged man wearing an Ethiopian robe. Some people say that the man is a singer from days past, a poet-prophet from the group known as the Ethiopians. Now he begins to chant out his verses, and the hand-drums follow him, backing him up. The akete, funde, bass. *Tak, tak, tak. Ga-bong, ga-bong, ga-bong. Boom, boom, boom.*

The robed one sings out a familiar tune:

I was born in the ghetto

Grew up in the ghetto

Learned that the cow jump over the moon

And that the dish run away with the spoon.

Where is I culture, where is I culture

Where is I culture?
The Chinaman come from China
The Indian belong to India
The whiteman come from Europe.
But I, a Ethiopian, I am here
Where is I culture?
I was born in the ghetto
Grew up in the ghetto
Learned that the cow jumped over the moon
And that the dish run away with the spoon
Where is I culture, where is I culture?

Normally, an American would not be permitted to hear any of this; nor would Europeans or Asians. It is strictly an African thing. In some inner circles of the Rasta movement, only dreadlocks (no "baldheads," or short-haired people, as they are still called) are permitted into the sacred circle, or the tabernacle, which is usually a bamboo and thatch structure.

Ernie, a "baldhead," comes over to me and says, "Back in the bush, the locks are the covenant. You see some men way back in there who wear nothing but thatch loincloth and carry gourdy with water. One time I went to a Nyabinghi where I was told by this dreadlock, 'If you love I, you must live I.' This meant that even though I was a Rasta, because I didn't wear the locks, I am not one of the brethren. I heard people say there that they didn't want any 'colored people' present, only blackman-Rastaman with dreadlocks."

Ernie concludes: "Jah never create just one kind of fish in the sea. All creatures come in different colors, since creation. That is how I see it. There are enough dreads in this business."

Then, taking a sip of ginger beer, he says, "There's the country dread, you know, the man in the hills. Old Rastas, usually, they dress in plain clothes, like you or me. We used to call them 'robbers' long ago because they looked like rough-tough people. I guess they had to be to live with all that prejudice put on them.

"Then there's the Nyabinghi dread, the kind that lives way, way up in the hills and wears just a little thatch cloth on the body, and not much else. They want no part of other people; they keep to themselves. They use no man-made utensils, cook only over the fire, eat only natural things."

Tipping his ginger beer, he finishes it.

"Boboshanti, you know, wear a wrap-head, which makes him look kind of Middle Eastern. This is a serious dread and hard working, as you must know. They don't care for reggae, or even this Nyabinghi. Normally, Bobo stay together, keeping their own counsel. But no one will mess with them. You see them on the road, carrying their thatch brooms that they sell, not bothering anybody—and nobody bothering them. Everyone know Bobo can handle himself, so not to mess with him."

Ernie laughs, and says, "There are as many kinds of Rastas as the reeds that grow on the riverbank. There's baldhead Rasta, like me. There's white Rasta, like you. There's rootical

Rasta—you know what I mean? Just rootsy people, who keep the faith, but don't believe in any ceremony, or chant, or Bible business. There's Congo Dread and Coptic Dread. But it all stem from the same thing, and it all go through the same place, the heart, you know."

Another speaker is now on the stage. This one is a woman with a turban on her head and a long African robe that covers her feet. She is very lovely and Nefertiti-looking, and she begins by speaking in bursts and moving her hands about in the air like wind-quick, golden brown butterflies.

"So much things to say, Bob Marley said, and I say it now too. So much things to say. I know that Bob say it true, but I also know in my heart that every man, woman, and child must say their say. Now my pickney ask me, Momma, what is the address of Jah? And I meditate upon this, but I have no answer that my pickney doesn't already know. So what do I say to her? What would you say? Where does Jah live now, my bretheren and sisteren? Then, last night, my little one come to me with a toothache; and all at once I see my answer, and say, 'There, right there, is where Jah live!' And my pickney learn the light of that truth. But, then, she ask a next question: 'Momma, what does it mean to be dead?' So, now, I flash an answer for this one, for it is as Bob has told us: Some who live are dead and some who are dead are alive. It is just so, I tell her. And this little daughter of mine, age four and a half, already know truth from lie, so I cannot hide anything from her—and why should I? Bretheren and sisteren, speak to your children, teach them well, always tell them the truth. Our posterity lies in the answer to their questions."

She finishes to a scattering of gentle applause. She walks offstage into the lowering firelight.

The greatest gift of Solomon was his insistence that wisdom comes from truth, and that truth comes out of the mouth. One must be true, therefore, to that truth. In Jamaica a person's bond is his word. As the man says in the following narrative, "Words are smoother than oil, softer than butter." The folk translation of this biblical expression is "honey works better than vinegar." Anything as sweet as honey and as soft as oil must be used with the greatest care.

We are in one of those north coast bars sometimes called tuck shops, because they are tucked into the hills, immersed in foliage. In the early morning as the mist rises, you see old grizzle-haired men from shilling-and-pence days stagger dizzily into the heat, listing to port, as they say, from too many white overproof rums, their voices loud and ungainly.

I am drinking a natural beverage called Supligen, supposedly a health drink made from malt. Next to me is a dreadlock, and beside him, a man who says that he was formerly a dread, but his locks were cut off during the seventies when "Babylon put up roadblocks and trim up a man's locks."

I ask if that happened often, the roadblock barbers from the police station. The baldhead Rasta replies, "Yes, mon, it

happen often. Babylon get vex wid us, want to put us off a
street, off a island, off a world. So me just seh, okay Babylon,
me nah need de lock dem. Me haffa go me own way, but
me nah need lock fe hold up me dignity."

The dreadlock next to us smiles, but makes no remark.
He is drinking a warm Red Stripe. His face is serious, his
eyes smiling. The baldhead observes my interest and comments, "It seh in de Bible, Render de 'eart, not de garment."
He raises a green bottle of the citrus soda, Ting, to his lips.
Then he takes a half-smoked Craven A cigarette from behind his ear and lights it. Drawing deeply, he exhales with
a sigh.

"Yes-I," he says. "De worl' change up, but stay de same."

"What goes around comes around," I say to him.

"Yes, mon. You 'ear a lot dese days 'bout outer-space,
inner-space, and all dem ting deh. But dere is only one space
inna dis worl'."

He taps his forehead and laughs. The dread, drinking the
warm Stripe, one small sip at a time, smiles again.

Outside, a car screeches to a stop, and a man yells in ping-
ing patois at the dreadlock, who turns his head slowly to
regard the caller. Still smiling, he leaves the bar, walking to
the little half-prime, half-paint Russian Lada, which is waiting for him.

This Rastaman is small, but he appears very strong. His
hair, natty-dreaded and shoulder-length, is pulled up and
tied back with a piece of twine, so that it is away from his
face and the back of his head. He slides cleanly into the open
door of the Lada.

"Yes, Ragga," the baldhead says before the car door closes, and the Lada careens away, spurting noxious blue exhaust that hangs on the roadside banana leaves.

I notice that the Rasta's beer is half-finished.

Turning around to the baldhead, I observe that his cigarette is snuffed out. A quarter plus filter remains, tucked back behind his ear. Everything in Jamaica is saved. The Red Stripe on the counter sits undisturbed, which indicates the man is coming right back to finish it—and he does, just as I am about to leave.

The baldhead remarks, "Is de brain, mon, dat tek deh astronaut into deh stars."

He grins, shaking the barstool with a loud guffaw.

"Deh brain," he repeats, pronouncing it, "deh bray-in."

I do not have to say anything—the man is fully wound, and he continues, "Man create him own destruction wid him brain. No ting on dis eart' come up new, every likkle ting been round since creation. Envy de spoiler since Cain, vanity de spoiler since Solomon. Every likkle ting, I tell you."

From behind us there is a shout. Tires squeal.

A bus, cutting the corner too close, has just bumped a man off his bicycle.

The bus is stopped, disgorging passengers. The bicyclist is on his side in the road, the bike on the ground next to him. A load of bananas, which the cyclist was carrying on his head, has been spilled everywhere.

I watch the bus driver come off the bus and help the cyclist to his feet. The driver says, "Sorry, sorry, Natty," for the cyclist is a Rastaman with small knotty dreads coiling off his head in all directions. He seems resigned, the dreadlock. He just gets back on his bike with the help of the driver.

"Nuttin' hurt, mon?" the driver calls.

He shakes his head. "Me all right, mon."

Passengers from the bus give him the bananas, which he hangs across the handlebars quite artfully, and he pedals off.

The incident is over—come and gone in a minute. The bus, back on track, grinds gears and goes away down the road.

I turn back to the bar. The smiley Rastaman has returned to finish his beer. The baldhead is moving off his bar stool.

He makes one last parting shot comment: "De words of a mon mout' smoother dan oil 'an softer dan butter."

"Yah, mon," I tell him. A bus coming in the opposite direction lurches to a stop. The baldhead, neatly dressed for work with shined brown shoes and crisp, pressed pants, hops on, holding the silver bar inside to stabilize the ride. The bus rolls ponderously up the grade towards Ocho Rios, and the man with whom I have been idling the time stares at me blankly, but it is a look that seems to say, "I know who you are."

And the bus is gone around the corner.

I finish the Supligen. The Rastaman, still sipping his beer, glances in my direction, then looks away. He has that cat's smile that never leaves his lips.

I pay for my drink and then offer to pay for the Rasta-man's beer. A small gesture in exchange for that life-affirming smile of his. He nods his acceptance—the smile remains set.

"Did you see the accident that just happened here?" I ask him as I am leaving.

"Yes, I saw it."

The Rastaman regards me with his narrow eyes, which are in contrast to the openness of the smile.

"In America," I tell him, "that would be a whole mess of lawsuits—a five-minute event can last five years in court."

"Well," he replies, swallowing off the last of the beer. "No harm done to the man."

"True. In America, though, there'd be a big lawsuit. The bicycle guy would get rich, and the bus driver would maybe lose his job. Naturally, the bus line would have to pay. But it would take years to determine this."

"I know the runnings," the Rastaman remarks. "Here inna Jamaica, the talk run smooth—what the mon say? Smoother than oil, softer than butter."

"In America, we say 'talk is cheap.'"

"When you use nice words, mon, you nice up the whole scene. Make it irie for everyone. No cheap talk, that. Nice, irie meditation; good talk. The bus driver say him sorry, sorry. So the mon don't get his feelings all mash up. Him feel okay."

The smile widens by a fraction.

He stands up and brushes his knuckles against mine. Then, hefting a little backpack over his shoulder, he touches my arm. "Easy, brother," he says, and walks off. I watch him disappear round the bend.

Bob Marley found himself, at the end of his life in 1981, and at the age of only thirty-six, a prophet in a strange land. The prophecy was peace. The tenor of the time was war. The land of which he prophesied was the world in which we live, our world. A world in torment.

The writing of Bob Marley is something new, yet something very old, as it comes almost directly from the Bible. However, like any great poet of any generation, Bob Marley drew from the sources that were close to his own roots. Thus his lyricism is fired with the trenchant imagery of the ghetto, the richness of Jamaican folk wisdom, and the love songs of the human heart.

His words are prophecy, poetry, and politics all in one, and they are listened to, not only by the ardent members of the Rastafarian movement, but by people of all nations, all colors, and creeds throughout the world. Particularly, however, Marley's music is aimed at uplifting the downpressed, as he put it, those souls whose suffering from the pressure of the neocolonial system is as hopeless now as it was unbearable in the 1970s. In effect, Marley was speaking to, for, and by himself because he knew, having come up from the ghetto as a youth, that human souls are ground into dust by the same self-serving iniquity that invented slavery. He wrote only of that which he truly "visioned." Today it is still topical, and will probably always remain so. Sixteen years after his death, his prophecy is prescient. The world, since his passing, is, if anything, more self-destructive.

And yet, although he realized that Armageddon seemed to be at hand, and that the human race was courting cataclysm, his own personal philosophy was one of hope. He believed that only through love, only through the hopeful heart, would the human race overcome its negative ways. He urged us, as individuals, regardless of race, religion, or politics, to come together and to love one another. In this he was not unlike Jesus of Nazareth, and Marley's pithy aphorisms, echoes of the New Testament, fully bear this out.

The life of Bob Marley was short and bright, flaring like an incandescent star. There is something in his sacrifice that suggests a kind of second coming; for as he reached out to help those who believed their burden was the heaviest, he drew nearer to the end of his own passage on earth.

He left us with an incomparable legacy of words. No poet of the people, no folk bard of the Caribbean ever produced more great, popular lyrics than did Bob Marley. His output was simply phenomenal, and it has barely been tapped. For this reason, he may be examined in the years to come not only as a charismatic singer but as a poet whose incendiary words are unequaled.

Indeed, it is in Marley's emerald phrases, his diamond images, his rephrasing of the Bible, that his greatness resides.

He studied the Bible, reading and reasoning with elders of the Rastafarian faith. But he did not stop there. He went on, carrying phrases in his head until they burst forth with astonishing clarity, mixed in, as they were, with the natural folk rhythms and patois patterns of Jamaica.

Not surprisingly, many of Bob Marley's words have a sharper edge than do the actual psalms, proverbs, and verses from which he drew inspiration. Using the Bible as a well of wisdom, he dipped in, and his dipper, like the great drinking gourd of African myth, came up sparkling.

The purpose of linking the words of Bob Marley with the verses of the Bible is twofold. First, it shows how clearly Marley interpreted the words of the elders, from Solomon of the Old Testament to Jesus of the New. Secondly, it challenges the reader to read and learn more. The Bible, whether viewed as literature or history, is a well that cannot run dry. Together, Marley's music and the Bible work in tandem as an education in Rastafarian thinking, a way of understanding the common denominator of a modern religion that refuses to be categorized.

Rasta is a way of life. Join hands and judge not. Go forward, as Bob Marley said, "through the roads of creation."

PROPHET

Of the many prophets of Rasta, there is only one who stands out as the cornerstone of today's faith. He is a man like Solomon, a man so gifted, so wise. He is compared with Joseph of Egypt. He is called the one who sits at the right hand of Selassie I. Bob Marley is named a prophet. His words ring true, spreading out across the ocean of nations. Here, then, is how Bob Marley took the sweet honey from the rock, the Bible and the oral teachings of the Ethiopian elders, which come from the Kebra Nagast, and made them his own.

JUDGE NOT

Judge not, before you judge yourself;
Judge not, if you're not ready for judgment.
The road of life is rocky and you may stumble, too;
so while you're talking about me
someone else is judging you.

BOB MARLEY

Judge not, that ye be not judged.
For with what judgment ye judge, ye shall be judged: and
with what measure ye mete,
it shall be measured to you again.

MATTHEW 7:1,2

STIFF-NECKED FOOLS

Destruction of the poor is in the poverty;
destruction of the soul is vanity.
The rich man's wealth is in his city;
the righteous wealth is in his holy place.

BOB MARLEY

The rich man's wealth is his strong city: the destruction of
the poor is their poverty.

PROVERBS 10:15

■

Stiff-necked fools, you think you are cool
to deny me for simplicity;
yes, you are gone, for so long
with your love of vanity.

BOB MARLEY

I said unto the fools, Deal not foolishly: and to the wicked,
Lift not up the horn: Lift not up your horn on high: speak
not with a stiff neck.

PSALM 75:4,5

BEND DOWN LOW

Bend down low, let me tell you what I know.
Fishermen row, you're going to reap what you sow.
BOB MARLEY

Even as I have seen, they that plow iniquity, and sow
wickedness, reap the same.
JOB 4:8

JUMP NYABINGHI

It remind I of the days in Jericho
when we trodden down Jericho walls;
these are the days when we trodden to Babylon;
gonna trodden, too, until Babylon falls.

BOB MARLEY

So the people shouted when the priests blew with the
trumpets: and it came to pass, when the people heard the
sound of the trumpet, and the people shouted with a great
shout, that the wall fell down flat, so that the people went
up into the city, every man straight before him, and they
took the city.

JOSHUA 6:20

GIVE THANKS AND PRAISES

Give thanks and praises to the moon and sky;
give thanks and praises so high.

BOB MARLEY

The day is thine, the night also is thine: thou has prepared
the light and the sun.

PSALMS 74:16

■

Noah had three sons: Ham, Shem, and Japheth;
and in Ham is known to be the prophet.

BOB MARLEY

And the sons of Noah, that went forth of the ark, were
Shem, and Ham, and Japheth: and Ham is the father of
Canaan. These are the three sons of Noah: and of them
was the whole earth overspread.

GENESIS 9:18,19

RASTAMAN LIVE UP

David slew Goliath with a sling and a stone;
Samson slew the Philistines with a donkey jawbone.

BOB MARLEY

So David prevailed over the Philistine with a sling and
with a stone, and smote the Philistine, and slew him; but
there was no sword in the hand of David.

I SAMUEL 17:50

And he found a new jawbone of an ass, and put forth his
hand, and took it, and slew a thousand men therewith.

JUDGES 15:15

WHO THE CAP FIT

Some will eat and drink with you,
then behind and suss upon you.
BOB MARLEY

He that dippeth his hand with me in the dish, the same
shall betray me.
MATTHEW 26:23

WE AND THEM

But in the beginning Jah created everything:
He gave man dominion over all thing.
But now it is too late, you see, men have lost their faith,
eating a pound of flesh from all the earth.

BOB MARLEY

And God said, Let us make man in our image, after our
likeness: and let them have dominion over the fish of the
sea, and over the fowl of the air, and over the cattle, . . .
and over every creeping thing that creepeth upon the earth.

GENESIS 2:26

FOREVER LOVING JAH

Just like a tree planted by the rivers of water
that bringeth forth fruit in due season;
every thing in life has its purpose,
find its reason, in every season.

BOB MARLEY

And he shall be like a tree planted by the rivers of water,
that bringeth forth his fruit in his season; his leaf also shall
not wither; and whatsoever he doeth shall prosper.

PSALM 1:3

ZION TRAIN

Don't gain the world and lose your soul;
wisdom is worth more than silver or gold.

BOB MARLEY

Happy is the man that findeth wisdom, and the man that
getteth understanding. For the merchandise of it is better
than the merchandise of silver, and the gain thereof than
fine gold.

PROVERBS 3:13,14

REAL SITUATION

Check out the real situation:
nation war against nation.
Where did it all begin?
Where will it end?
Well, it seems like total destruction
the only solution.

BOB MARLEY

For nation shall rise against nation, and kingdom against
kingdom: and there shall be earthquakes in diverse places,
and there shall be famines and troubles: these are the
beginnings of sorrows.

MARK 13:8

REDEMPTION SONG

How long shall they kill our prophets
while we stand aside and look?
Some say it's just a part of it,
we have to fulfill the book.

BOB MARLEY

Wherefore, behold, I send unto you prophets, and wise
men, and scribes: and some of them ye shall kill and
crucify; and some of them shall ye scourge in your
synagogues, and persecute them from city to city.

MATTHEW 24:34

And ye shall hear of wars and rumors of wars: see that ye
be not troubled: for all these things must come to pass, but
the end is not yet.

MATTHEW 24:6

SMALL AXE

You are working iniquity to achieve vanity...
But the goodness of Jah Jah I-dureth for-Iver.

BOB MARLEY

He that soweth iniquity shall reap vanity: and the rod of
his anger shall fail.

PROVERBS 22:8

■

Whosoever diggeth a pit shall fall in it;
whosoever diggeth a pit shall bury in it.

BOB MARLEY

Whoso diggeth a pit shall fall therein; and he that rolleth a
stone, it will return upon him.

PROVERBS 22:8

PASS IT ON

What is in the darkness must be brought to light.

BOB MARLEY

Therefore whatsoever ye have spoken in darkness shall be heard in the light.

LUKE 12:3

RASTAMAN CHANT

And I hear the angel with the seventh seal,
Babylon, your throne gone down.
BOB MARLEY

And when he had opened the seventh seal, there was
silence in heaven.
REVELATION 8:1

RIDE NATTY RIDE

The stone that the builder refuse
shall be the head corner stone;
and no matter what game they play,
we've got something they can never take away.

BOB MARLEY

The stone which the builders refused is become the head
stone of the corner.

PSALM 118:22

AMBUSH IN THE NIGHT

See them fighting for power,
but they know not the hour.

BOB MARLEY

Watch therefore, for ye know neither the day nor the hour.

MATTHEW 25:13

WAKE UP AND LIVE

We are more than sand on the seashore;
we're more than numbers.

BOB MARLEY

If I should count them, they are more in number than the sand.

PSALM 139:18

BABYLON SYSTEM

We have been trodding on the wine press much too long...
BOB MARLEY

The treaders shall tread out no wine in their presses; I
have made their vintage shouting to cease.
ISAIAH 16:10

SURVIVAL

We are survivors like Shadrach, Meshach, and Abednego;
go in the fire but they never get burned.

BOB MARLEY

Then Shadrach, Meshach, and Abednego came forth of the
midst of the fire . . . nor was a hair of their head singed,
neither were their coats changed, nor the smell of fire had
passed on them.

DANIEL 3:26,27

■

A good man is never honored in his own land.

BOB MARLEY

A prophet is not without honour, but in his own country.

MARK 6:4

GUILTINESS

Woe to the downpressor, they eat the bread of sorrow;
woe to the downpressor, they eat the bread of sad tomorrow.

BOB MARLEY

It is vain for you to rise up early, to sit up late, to eat the
bread of sorrows.

PSALM 127:2

THE HEATHEN

As a man sows, so shall he reap.

BOB MARLEY

They that plow iniquity, and sow wickedness, reap the same.

JOB 4:8

EXODUS

Exodus, movement of Jah people . . .
send us another brother Moses
going to cross the Red Sea.

BOB MARLEY

So Moses brought Israel from the Red Sea, and they went
out into the wilderness.

EXODUS 15:22

IRON LION ZION

Iron like a lion in Zion;
iron like a lion in Zion;
iron, lion, Zion.

The young lion roaring on his prey ... so shall the Lord of
Hosts come down to fight for Mount Zion.

ISAIAH 31:4

NATURAL MYSTIC

This could be the first trumpet,
might as well be the last;
many more will have to suffer,
many more will have to die;
don't ask me why.

BOB MARLEY

And the first voice which I heard was as it were of a
trumpet talking with me; which said, Come up hither, and
I will show thee things which must be hereafter.

REVELATION 4:1

BIBLIOGRAPHY

Asimov, Isaac. *Asimov's Guide to the Bible*. New York: Wings Books, 1969.

Barrett, Leonard. *The Rastafarians*. Boston: Beacon Press, 1977.

Bloom, Harold, and David Rosenberg. *The Book of J*. New York: Grove Weidenfeld, 1990.

Bob Marley Foundation. *Songs of Freedom: A Discography*. Kingston, Jamaica, 1993.

Bob Marley Songs of Freedom Songbook. Wisconsin: Hal Leonard Publishing Corporation, 1992.

Book, The. Wheaton, Ill.: Tynedale House Publishers, 1984.

Boot, Adrian, Chris Salewicz, and Rita Marley, ed. *Bob Marley: Songs of Freedom*. New York: Viking Studio Books, 1995.

Brooks, Miguel. *Kebra Negast: The Glory of the Kings*. Kingston, Jamaica: Kingston Publishers, Ltd., 1995.

Bryan, Patrick, and Rupert Lewis. *Garvey: His Work and Impact*. Kingston, Jamaica: University of the West Indies, 1988.

Budge, E. A. *The Queen of Sheba and Her Only Son Menyelek*. London: Medici Society, 1922.

Charles, R. H. *The Book of Enoch*. London: Society for the Promotion of Christian Knowledge, 1917.

Davis, Stephen. *Reggae Bloodlines: In Search of the Music and Culture of Jamaica*. New York: Anchor Press, 1979.

Faristzaddi, Millard. *Itations of Jamaica and I Rastafari*. Miami: Judah Anbesa, 1987.

Harris, J. Rendel. *The Odes and Psalms of Solomon*. London: Cambridge University Press, 1909.

Hausman, Gerald, and Kelvin Rodriques. *African-American Alphabet*. New York: St. Martin's Press, 1996.

The Holy Bible. King James Version.

Insight Guides to Jamaica. New Jersey: Prentice Hall, 1984.

Lorenz, Konrad. *King Solomon's Ring*. New York: Thomas Crowell & Co., 1952.

Lunta, Karl. *Jamaica Handbook*. California: Moon Publishers, 1993.

McCann, Ian. *In His Own Words*. London: Omnibus Press, 1993.

McCray, Reverend Walter Arthur. *The Black Presence in the Bible*. Chicago, Ill.: Black Light Fellowship, 1995.

Nicholas, Tracy. *Rastafari: A Way of Life*. New York: Anchor Press/Doubleday, 1979.

Owens, Joseph. *Dread*. Kingston, Jamaica: Sangster Publishers, 1976.

Patterson, Orlando. *Children of Sisyphus*. London: Longman Publishers, 1964.

Senior, Olive. *A-Z of Jamaican Heritage*. Kingston, Jamaica: The Gleaner Co., 1988.

Smith, William. *Smith's Bible Dictionary*. New York: Jove Books, 1977.

Tafari, Jabulani I. *A Rastafari View of Marcus Mosiah Garvey*. Kingston, Jamaica: GreatCompany JA Ltd., 1996.

Talamon, Bruce, and Roger Steffens. *Bob Marley: Spirit Dancer*. New York, London: W. W. Norton, 1994.

White, Timothy. *Catch a Fire: The Life of Bob Marley*. New York: Henry Holt, 1989.

INDEX

"... my mother's children ...
made me the keeper of
the vineyards...

~Song of Solomon 1:6

The Ancestral Tree

embracing

Adam, Solomon,

and

Haile Selassie

Bathsheba

Adramis

Rehoboam

Amisa

Solomon

Sheba

Jochim

Hanna

Bayna-Lehkem (Menyelek)

Cain

Joseph

Mary

Haile Selassie

Eve

Jesus